Dear Reader

The book you are [holding] [is helping] [thousands] of men find deeper significance and lead more balanced lives. This special edition copy of *Devotions for the Man in the Mirror* is part of a unique effort to distribute copies to men throughout the world.

A number of men made sacrifices for you to receive this book. Why would they do that? They sacrificed because the gospel has changed their lives.

We live in busy, stressful times. I believe a regular time in your day or week to ponder God's Word and his promises will be of great benefit to you. My dream is that by reading it you will find contentment and a success that really matters.

Patrick Morley
Founder & CEO
Man in the Mirror
www.maninthemirror.org

BOOKS BY PATRICK MORLEY

Coming Back to God
The Dad in the Mirror (coauthored with David Delk)
Devotions for Couples
Devotions for the Man in the Mirror
Discipleship for the Man in the Mirror
The Man in the Mirror
Second Half for the Man in the Mirror
Seven Seasons of the Man in the Mirror
Ten Secrets for the Man in the Mirror
Understanding Your Man in the Mirror
The Young Man in the Mirror

THE MAN IN THE MIRROR LIBRARY

DEVOTIONS
for the MAN *in the* MIRROR

Formerly titled *Walking with Christ in the Details of Life*

**57 READINGS TO CULTIVATE A
DEEPER WALK WITH CHRIST**

PATRICK MORLEY

ZONDERVAN™

GRAND RAPIDS, MICHIGAN 49530 USA

ZONDERVAN™

Devotions for the Man in the Mirror
Formerly titled *Walking with Christ in the Details of Life*
Copyright © 1990, 1992, and 1998 by Patrick M. Morley

Requests for information should be addressed to:
Zondervan, *Grand Rapids, Michigan 49530*

ISBN 0-310-25722-0

Published in association with the literary agency of Wolgemuth & Associates, Inc.

Printed in the United States of America

04 05 06 07 08 09 /❖ OP/ 10 9 8 7 6 5 4 3 2 1

To my wife, Patsy,
the best Christian I know.
A gentle, kind person,
she understands the surrendered life.

Contents

PART SIX: THE TOOLS OF SURRENDER

PART SEVEN: RESPONDING TO THE STRUGGLES OF DAILY LIFE

Part Eight: Developing My Personal Character

Acknowledgments

I would like to express heartfelt gratitude to Ken Moar for the hundreds of hours over the past thirteen years we have spent together talking—sometimes muddling—through the issues of leading a surrendered life.

A special thank you to my wife, Patsy, and my pastor, Dr. H. Charles Green, for proofing the manuscript for clarity in its telling, accuracy in its meaning, and compassion in its applying.

Introduction

"God opposes the proud but gives grace to the humble."
Submit yourselves, then, to God. Resist the devil and
he will flee from you. Come near to God and he will
come near to you.

James 4:6–8

After a storybook romance, Jim swept Sandy into what all observers believed would be the idyllic kind of life found in an especially good novel.

Jim dedicated himself to the task of conquering the corporate world, an endeavor which consumed long hours—his best hours. Sandy devoted herself to the strenuous task of raising the two perfectly beautiful children which they promptly brought into the world.

One morning, while Jim was dressing for an early morning meeting, Sandy calmly told him, "Jim, I don't love you any more. I filed papers for a divorce yesterday."

In my office, a broken-hearted Jim sighed heavily as he explained how they both had been doing their "own thing" ever since the first day back from their honeymoon.

"Does Sandy have a Christian life view?" I asked. A long, quizzical pause followed.

"I'm not sure I understand what you mean," Jim cautiously responded.

"I know that Sandy is a Christian, Jim. But what I'm asking is different. Does Sandy have a distinctly Christian way of looking at things? In other words, when she has a problem to solve, a plan to develop, a priority to set, or a decision to make, does she think about these things Christianly—does she have a Christian life view?"

After another protracted pause, Jim slowly responded, "Well, no, now that you put it that way, I would have to say no, I don't think she does."

The Man in the Mirror concluded with a comment on "the sin of partial surrender." And that's where I would like to pick up and go on for men and women alike. It is the sin of Jim and Sandy, and of countless others of us, too.

THE PROBLEM

The *partially surrendered life* may be Christian in spirit, but it is secular in practice. It may save one's soul, but it hardly leaves a noticeable ripple on one's lifestyle, life view, or the world and culture in which we live. Of what earthly value is Christianity if it leaves no indelible mark on one's lifestyle? It is of no value (in this life) to be Christian if you do not think Christianly—if you do not have a Christian life view.

We live in a broken generation. One doesn't need to be a rocket scientist to make this observation, but the obvious question, of course, is *Why?* Many think the answer is confusing, but it is not. It is found throughout the record of Scripture—it is *disobedience*. It is to lead a partially surrendered life; or worse, an unsurrendered, unyielded life. How can we learn how to be obedient? We must learn how to surrender, to submit to Christ in the details of daily life.

Over the past few decades, many of us started off on the wrong foot with Jesus Christ. It is the proposition

that Jesus can be *Savior* without being *Lord*. It is the idea
that one can *add* Christ, but not *subtract* sin. Many of us
have merely added Christ to our lives as another interest
in an already busy and otherwise over-crowded schedule.
This sort of thinking has watered down the meaning of
a personal relationship with Christ.

The problem is that we often seek the God we want,
but do not know the God who is. Many men and women
I have met express complete, utter frustration about leading this kind of defeated (sometimes counterfeit), partially surrendered life—the life of a cultural Christian.

How did this come about? The *low demands* of cultural Christianity have led to a *low response*—it has
become the norm. But the Bible calls men and women to
a *turning point*, to a radical, life-transforming change.
This turning point is no mean challenge, but a full surrender to history's most ideal, most radical leader: the
Lord Jesus Christ.

Have you *fully* surrendered to the God who is, or are
you still seeking the God you want? Have you reached
your turning point? If you have, or if you sense a desire
to, *Devotions for the Man in the Mirror* is for you. I wrote
Devotions for the Man in the Mirror as a user-friendly book
of daily readings to help each of us negotiate the terms of
a more full, more total, more complete, no regrets surrender to Christ.

THE MEANING OF FULL SURRENDER

What does it mean to fully surrender to Christ? To
fully surrender to Christ doesn't mean to become a
recluse, but a reformer; not a monk, but a manager; not
a loner, but a leader. A Biblical surrender is a thinking
surrender, carefully carved by thoughtful self-examination and submission to Christ.

To surrender is to be so completely preoccupied with Christ that you hunger for your life to reflect His life as though in a mirror. No one, of course, will achieve a true full surrender in this life, but that in no way negates His call on us to be perfect. Jesus said, "'Be perfect, therefore, as your heavenly Father is perfect'" (Matthew 5:48).

The goal of surrender, simply stated, is to be conformed to the likeness (or image) of Christ (see Romans 8:29), not as an exercise which leads to bondage, but to apprehend the true freedom that only Jesus offers. The irony of surrender is a paradox; it is a seeming contradiction that on further investigation is actually no contradiction at all.

Surrender means not only that we surrender to something, but also that we surrender from some things. For that reason we will spend time not only on the vector our lives should take, but also on how to escape the worldly life we must learn to leave behind.

To surrender is to abandon the *comfortable orbit*—the life of the cultural Christian. It is not to drop out; it is not an excuse for mediocrity. To fully surrender means to be so completely dependent upon Christ that obedience brands your behavior.

Why do most miss out on this surrendered life? Human nature works on every one us to find "the comfortable orbit." When we first trust Christ, we draw close to the Light to feel His warmth, but soon we notice the brilliant beams of light pulsate like powerful strobes that expose every minute blemish in our character. It's hard to take the heat, so we often make a retreat.

To retreat too far from the Light, though, leaves us chilly—it's cold out there. So we explore until we find a nice, warm zone to comfortably orbit around the Light, not too close, not too far away. Not cold, but not on fire either. And you hate it; you are miserable. You want to be on fire for Christ, to trust Him completely, to obey, to live out of the overflow of an abundant life, filled with purpose and meaning.

If you are ready to recklessly abandon the comfortable orbit, if you are ready to negotiate the terms of a full surrender with the Lord, then welcome to *Devotions for the Man in the Mirror.*

HOW TO READ THIS BOOK

I suggest you read one chapter (or even a few) at a time. You can do this daily or maybe a couple of days each week. Perhaps you could leave the book on your nightstand for easy access and as a quiet reminder. Except for the anecdotes, I encourage you to read meditatively and reflect on things that strike you as interesting. Pray before reading and ask God to illumine some nugget of truth and an application to you personally.

If you are weary of living a partially surrendered life, or if you long for a deeper personal walk with Christ, then welcome to *Devotions for the Man in the Mirror.* I wrote this book for you. I pray these pages will help you negotiate the terms of a more full, total, complete surrender to Christ.

PART ONE

The God We Want Versus the God Who Is

There is a God we want, and there is a God who is—and they are not the same God.

ONE

The Kingdom:
Temporal Kingdoms

Your kingdom come, your will be done.

Matthew 6:10

Goodyear. Rockefeller. Pulitzer. Vanderbilt. Morgan. Macy. Gould. Crane. Astor. These celebrated millionaires represented only the most highly visible names from the membership rolls of the powerful Jekyll Island Club.

In 1886 some of the East Coast's most prominent millionaires purchased a coastal island near Georgia for a hunting preserve and winter family retreat. By the early 1900s, members had informally linked together to form one of the most powerful, wealthy, and influential earthly kingdom ever known.

Members of the exclusive, clannish Jekyll Island Club controlled one-sixth of the world's wealth, forging together an alliance that virtually controlled America's corporations and government—the railroads, the banks, the industrial complex, the significant inventions.

To understand how vast this power was, consider these examples: In the early 1900s, J. P. Morgan twice financed the teetering United States government, staving off federal bankruptcy. On another occasion, at a clandestine meeting in one of the elegant private meeting rooms at the secluded Jekyll Island Clubhouse, top government officials hammered out the first draft of the Federal Reserve Act.

The first transcontinental telephone call was initiated from the Jekyll Island Clubhouse to President Woodrow Wilson in Washington and Alexander Graham Bell in New York. The concentration of power at the Jekyll Island Club represented the zenith to which men can orchestrate temporal kingdoms.

Today, the Jekyll Island Club is history. Curious visitors wander among a half-dozen restored buildings scattered around the grounds. The overgrowth of weeds, the peeling paint, the shattered glass—all symbols of the futility of man-made kingdoms. Except those restored for tourists, the posh winter "cottages" lay in ruin, betraying the brief standing given to the temporal kingdoms of man.

Though they once commanded one-sixth of the world's wealth, these power brokers have two things in common with every other man of their era: All their plans have come and gone, and they are all dead. "What good will it be for a man if he gains the whole world, yet forfeits his soul?" (Matthew 16:26).

All the benefits of prosperity are temporal. All the risks of prosperity are eternal. No matter how affluent and influential we become in the prosperous, material world, we will not find eternal profit from temporal kingdoms. Despite all our prosperity, we must still come daily to the foot of the Cross of the Lord Jesus Christ to inherit an eternal kingdom.

That is why the first supplication that Jesus taught us, His disciples, was, "your kingdom come, your will be done on earth as it is in heaven." Tread lightly in temporal kingdoms, for all our plans will come to an end, and then we die. The only profit that matters is an eternal one.

I Surrender

Our Father in heaven, hallowed be Your name, Your kingdom come *in my life*, Your will be done *in my life*, here and now, on earth, as it is in heaven. I surrender to You the temporal kingdom I have been building. Give me, I pray, the eternal kingdom. Amen.

TWO

Jesus: A Case of Mistaken Identity

"But what about you?" he asked. *"Who do you say I am?"*

Matthew 16:15

For several years two dozen men, half black and half white, met on Saturday morning once each month. A racial disturbance in our city had prompted both groups of us to ask the same questions, "Who are these people, and how can we know them?" So we started meeting to find some answers. Our purpose was not to change the city, but to change ourselves, to learn how to love one another.

One day at lunch three of us were discussing an issue. The confident, radiant demeanor of one of the men, a black pastor, commanded respect. During our conversation, however, he made a radical statement about remaining patient that seemed out of character. Immediately, the two of us jumped on him like a dog on a bone.

He slowly turned his eyes to explore each of our faces; then he began to speak, deliberate and restrained.

In the next few minutes he revealed an astonishing addition to my understanding of who he was.

"When I arrived at my first church," he began, "weed had taken the place over. The building was in shambles. Five pastors had come and gone in three years. No one in the community had any confidence that I would be any different, so no one came to worship.

"My wife and I patched and painted and replaced the broken windows. Over time we restored the church building to a functional state. I made calls around the community, but still no one seemed the least bit interested.

"So, not knowing exactly what to do, I decided to prepare and preach my sermons as if the place was full. Every Sunday morning I stepped into the pulpit and preached my best sermons to empty pews—completely empty pews except for my wife. Every Sunday for three years I preached as though the place was packed, but in reality it was still empty.

"Finally, after three strained years, God gave us one family. He became my Sunday School superintendent— his kids were the only ones we had in Sunday School. Slowly, over the next few months, however, God began to bless. He rewarded my faithfulness all those years. My preaching to an empty church may not have been smart, but it was faithful; I was patient, and I persevered."

By now my friend and I had melted into an embarrassed puddle of humbled awe. We had questioned his radical statement about patience. The real lesson for the day was about jumping to conclusions, about not taking time to know the true identity of one we called our friend.

We thought we knew the true identity of this black pastor. We had taken the little we knew, projected it, and come to the wrong conclusion. He was more than what he appeared to be. Isn't everyone more than what they first appear to be?

During His year of popularity, Jesus asked his disciples one day, "Who do people say the Son of Man is?"

"They replied, 'Some say John the Baptist; others say Elijah; and still others, Jeremiah or one of the Prophets'" (Matthew 16:13–14).

Of course, Jesus already knew who the people thought He was. They thought He was anyone and everyone except who He really was. It was a case of mistaken identity. The people took what little they knew of Jesus and came to the wrong conclusion. He was more than He appeared to be.

Then Jesus queried his disciples. "'But what about you?' he asked. 'Who do you say I am?'"

"Simon Peter answered, 'You are the Christ, the Son of the living God'" (Matthew 16:16).

As Peter learned more of this remarkable man, his respect turned to awe. Then he humbled himself, confessing Him to be the Messiah, the Christ. Peter learned the true identity of Jesus, not just a good man, not just a prophet, not just a moral teacher, or a man of prayer, or a priest, but "the Christ, the Son of the living God" (v. 16).

Jesus was the long awaited Messiah, the Lamb of God that takes away the sins of the world. He was far more than He first appeared. The people had mistaken His identity. Still do. "But what about you? Who do you say I am?" (v. 15).

Are you sure of His real identity? Have you assumed too little—or too much—about who He is? Do you understand His character? Don't get caught in a case of mistaken identity.

Know the Jesus who is, not the Jesus you want. Yes, He is a moral teacher, a prophet, and a priest. But He is also the King, the Eternal Creator, the Father, the Christ, the Son of the living God. Know Him as He really is, be humbled by the revelation of His true identity, and worship Him, Christ the King.

I SURRENDER

Jesus, you are the Christ, the Son of the living God. I am often guilty of mistaking Your identity. I suspect I have thought too narrowly of You. I have held to my perceptions of who You are, and who I want You to be. Help me to know You as You really are, not as I perceive You to be. Amen.

THREE

Revival: The Gospel of Addition

I preached that they should repent and turn to God and prove their repentance by their deeds.

Acts 26:20

Over the past few years I have heard several mature, respected Christian leaders remark that God was not saying very much back in the 1950s. If He was silent then, His voice virtually thundered in the sixties, seventies, and eighties. In those decades America underwent a revival of unparalleled historic proportion.

According to Gallup surveys, confirmed by other polls taken over the past fifteen years, 33 percent of all Americans over age eighteen indicate they are evangelical or "born again" Christians. That translates into 59 million Christians, or one in every three adults, who experienced a turning point in their lives as they made a personal commitment to Jesus Christ.

This information should grip us with terror. It means that the greatest revival in history has so far been impotent to change society. It's *revival* without *reforma-*

tion. It's a revival which left the country floundering in spiritual ignorance. It's a change in *belief* without a corresponding change in *behavior*.

Other polls, as well as our own experience, show that this dramatic *spiritual* conversion has not been followed by a *moral* conversion. Instead, during those decades the moral will and character of America fractured into thousands of diverse, dwarfish, self-determined systems of values and beliefs.

Those value/belief systems commingled with an historical Judeo-Christian ethic, but mostly they built on the footings of the moral disillusionment of the times:

- The suspicious sixties: "Down with the establishment!" Vietnam. Watts.
- The selfish seventies: "You can have it all." Watergate.
- The alienated eighties: "Go for it." "If it feels good, do it!"

We preached a gospel relevant to our times, one that was in agreement with what contemporary society was saying.

THE AMERICAN GOSPEL

How did the building blocks of the gospel become glued together with the cement of self-centeredness? The American gospel has evolved into a gospel of addition without subtraction. It is the belief that we can add Christ to our lives, but not subtract sin. It is a change in belief without a change in behavior. It is a spiritual experience without any cultural impact. It is revival without reformation. It is revival without repentance.

Though illogical at first blush, a closer examination shows how this happened. When a company experiences a burst in sales, it redirects its energy and resources into capturing those sales while the window of opportunity is cracked open. The natural consequence? The back office stutters and sputters.

In a similar way, Christianity experienced an enormous burst in sales (read: evangelism). And the Christian world appropriately poured its energy and resources into capitalizing on the window God cracked open. But the back office (read: discipleship) has stuttered and sputtered. The result? We live in a nation of spiritual stutterers and sputterers—spiritual infants.

Every new generation of believers must be discipled. Once shown how to add Christ to their lives, they must be taught how to subtract sin—and to obey. Paul's gospel was adamant that adding Jesus must be accompanied by subtracting sin. "I preached that they should repent [subtract sin] and turn to God [add Christ] and prove their repentance by their deeds [obedience]." Have you added Christ to your life without subtracting sin?

The *proof* of religious conversion is to demonstrate that we have both added a relationship with Christ and that we have subtracted sin (repentance). And we multiply proof to a weary world by what we do—our deeds, our obedience. What we do must confirm what we say. Our deeds are the proof of our repentance. Are you proving your repentance to the world by your deeds?

A changed life is one that has added Christ and subtracted sin, that attracts a world weary of worn-out words. Obedience is the proof. Paul labeled his mission "to call people . . . to the obedience that comes from faith" (Romans 1:5). Paul knew that unless the believer became a "behave-er" that revival would not lead to a reformed life.

Are you obedient? Is there a difference between your behavior and those around you who have never met the Savior? If there is none, what will attract them to the kingdom of God?

Are you a disciple of Christ, or still an infant? Learn why Paul "preached that they should repent and turn to God and prove their repentance by their deeds." What is it that Paul saw that today's Christian has not yet seen? Do you see it yet?

I Surrender

Lord Jesus, I see it. I see that I have added You to my life, but that I have not subtracted sin as You desire I should. Your gospel is the gospel of addition and subtraction—love and holiness. Deep in my soul I desire to repent, to add You at a new level of full surrender, and to prove my repentance by what I do—by how I behave. Fill me with the power of the Holy Spirit so that I can demonstrate a changed life to a weary world. Amen.

FOUR

Worship: Our Attitude Toward God

"You are worthy, our Lord and God, to receive glory and honor and power, for you created all things, and by your will they were created and have their being."

Revelation 4:11

Nearly everyone has had the experience of meeting someone particularly dignified, but in a quiet, unassuming sort of way. That person doesn't say much about himself, yet he projects an incandescent, warm self-confidence.

He seems so genuinely interested in you that you speak freely and openly with him in the casual, familiar every-day talk you use at home or with close friends—the kind you would never use around your boss or pastor.

Only later, you learn the person with whom you spoke is an important industrialist, a distinguished diplomat, or a celebrated speaker. When the breadth of his accomplishments becomes known to you, your attitude changes sharply. You would never again speak to that person with such casually chosen words, expressing such capricious thoughts. The next time, if there would ever be a next time, you would rehearse every word carefully before you spoke. You would carefully frame each thought to show the respect due such an important person.

Why is it, then, that we display such a casual, even capricious, attitude when speaking to Him who "created all things," and through whom all things have their being?

Our family once attended a tawdry, gimmicky religious meeting. As the minutes painfully ticked away, I slumped deeper and deeper into my chair. The meeting organizers created a freakish, carnival-like atmosphere, like a side-show off the midway. The barker hawked religious souvenirs with Brother Love's zeal. I couldn't help but wonder, *Would they be a little bit embarrassed if they learned Jesus had sat on the front row?*

If we ponder who God really is before we carelessly utter any remark before or about Him, surely we will render a more considered, respectful utterance. This is no different from the respect we would show the distinguished stranger if we knew their true identity. When once we see Him as He really is, the trite or casual remark no longer seems appropriate.

In fact, when we know the God who is, our first reaction is to hide from the awfulness of His presence. We want to see the face of God, until the presence of His glory draws near. Then, we want Him to hide us in the cleft of a rock. His presence is like peals of thunder and the fierce winds of a violent storm, and we reconsider the foolishness of our whim to see Him. He is a holy God. Not only holy—but holy, holy, holy. "Holy, holy, holy is the Lord God Almighty, who was, and is, and is to come" (Revelation 4:8).

THE CUE FROM "OTHER" CREATED BEINGS

In heaven one hundred million loyal angels will encircle the throne of God and sing in a loud voice, "Worthy is the Lamb, who was slain, to receive power and wealth and wisdom and strength and honor and glory and praise!" (Revelation 5:12). The four living creatures, those beings allowed closest to His throne say, "Holy, holy, holy." The elders who sit on the twenty-four thrones which surround the throne cry out, "You are worthy."

After that "every creature in heaven and on earth and under the earth and on the seas, and all that is in them" will sing, "To him who sits on the throne and to the Lamb be praise and honor and glory and power, for ever and ever!" (Revelation 5:13). You and I will be "every creature."

Let us reconsider who God is—His power, His wealth, His wisdom, His glory, His honor, His praise. Let us take our cue from the living creatures, the elders, and the angels. Let us not approach the God who is holy, holy, holy with caprice or unthinking casualness.

Let us come into His presence with praise and thanksgiving, but also in sober recognition that we are in the presence of the Holy. "Let us then approach the throne of grace with confidence" (Hebrews 4:16), but with the bearing and respect we would show to the One whose identity we have learned: the God who is, who created all things, in whom we have our being.

When you come apart to meet with God consider these statements as you begin your time in His presence. Pause and meditate upon them:

- Father, I come to meet with You.... Meet with me.
- Lord Jesus, I come to meet with You....
  Meet with me.
- Holy Spirit, I come to meet with You....
  Meet with me.

Enter into the presence of the God who is with the respect and honor and praise He is due. Do it as you would when you learn the identity of the dignified stranger.

I Surrender

Father, my attitude has been capricious and overly casual. I have not shown you the respect due Your name. I abandon the specious ways in which I have spoken to You. I humble myself. Hide me in a cleft in the rock so that I will not perish when Your glory passes by me. I surrender my unthinking attitude toward the privilege of entering the holiness of Your presence. Amen.

PART TWO

The Escape from Cultural Christianity

Cultural Christianity means to pursue the God we want instead of the God who is. It is the tendency to be shallow in our understanding of God, wanting Him to be more of a gentle grandfather type who spoils us and lets us have our own way. It is sensing a need for God, but on our own terms. It is wanting the God we have underlined in our Bibles without wanting the rest of Him, too. It is God relative instead of God absolute.

From *The Man in the Mirror*

The largest denomination in Western civilization is cultural Christianity.

Carl Hallberg

FIVE

Prosperity: A Gift of God

Moreover, when God gives any man wealth and possessions, and enables him to enjoy them, to accept his lot and to be happy in his work—this is a gift of God.

Ecclesiastes 5:19

The meeting broke up, and the three of us made our way toward the parking lot. The other two men unlocked expensive luxury cars and slipped inside onto soft, hand-crafted leather seats. As their engines cranked, rows of luminous dials and gauges blinked and sputtered to life in the cockpits.

One of these men is a believer; the other is not. For the one who is not, his automobile represented the apex of his achievements. It symbolized his human potential; it discreetly certified his prosperity to the world around him. His car was the icon of his identity. It represented the end to which he aspired.

The believer appreciated the quality of the car he drove. God had blessed his life with prosperity, yet a sense of guilt lingered about the abundance of his life—especially when compared to many of the struggling saints in his church.

He ran the company he owned on Christian principles—not as a "Christian" company with a big Bible positioned pretentiously on the reception table, but one which held integrity and ethical behavior as its highest values. He employed several people, enabling them to support their families. His own behavior influenced many employees to trust Christ as their own Savior and Lord.

He shared regularly with the poor and spread good works throughout his community. He was leaving the world a better place, a more spiritual place. His life was a testimony to Christ. Still, guilt over his prosperity lingered, haunting his thoughts. He had never been able to accept his lot in life and, as a consequence, he didn't enjoy his possessions. He missed the gift of God.

THE PURPOSE OF PROSPERITY

What is the purpose of prosperity? God owns everything. He searches for men and women to whom He can entrust the material world He owns. Pagans cut throats as they compete for their slice of the prosperity pie. But the hand of God bestows prosperity on certain of His children without trouble. He does so exclusively to extend the kingdom of God in the temporal world. He hides no secret reason.

What happens to the one—believer or unbeliever— who misses the purpose of prosperity, who ignores the mandate to extend the kingdom of God? He does not please the Lord, and the blessing will be taken away. "To the man who pleases him, God gives wisdom, knowledge and happiness, but to the sinner he gives the task of gathering and storing up wealth to hand it over to the one who pleases God" (Ecclesiastes 2:26). Has God blessed you materially? Virtually every reader will fall in the category of financially blessed, especially on a world standard. Today, two of three people live in hunger worldwide. Though blessed, we tend to err with our prosperity. What common errors do people make with money?

THE FOUR ERRORS OF PROSPERITY

Financially blessed Christians often fall for one or more of four great errors.

1. *Taking Credit for Prosperity.* The foremost error, when error exists, is for believers to ascribe credit for their success to themselves. Their possessions become the apex of their achievements, the icon of their identity, the end to which they aspire. They might as well be pagans, for God detests idol worship.

2. *Ingratitude for Prosperity.* The second great error is to receive the blessing of God without gratitude. The enemy is never more happy than when he confounds a financially blessed believer to take their blessing for granted. They don't take credit, but neither do they give God credit. Pause for perspective often. Don't live myopically; thank God for your blessing.

3. *Guilt over Prosperity.* The third great error belongs to those who feel the sting of guilt from financial abundance. They find accepting their lot in life difficult. Satan poisons their spirit from experiencing the joy and peace of God. He clouds every abundant experience with a heavy shroud of guilt. You must realize God is at the root of your blessing. Instead of feeling guilt over abundance, find God's purpose for it. Be grateful, not guilty.

4. *Dependence upon Prosperity.* The fourth great error believers make is to depend on their prosperity, not

Christ. Stored wealth is the dead giveaway for this error. To trust in the size of your bank balance is what financial counselor and author Ron Blue terms "over-accumulation."

Accumulating any more than the amount needed to retire, to go into full-time Christian service, to perpetuate a business, and/or to provide for children's education is accumulating too much.

The wheels of Christianity grind at an enormous price. God blessed you so that you will bless His work. It is not for you only, but for the work of the kingdom of God. Don't use prosperity to only increase your lifestyle; extend the kingdom of God. Enjoy your prosperity gratefully and multiply the work of God.

Don't lose the gift of God. Please Him. Don't miss the purpose of your prosperity. Prosperity is from God, not for you only, but as a means to other ends—the ends of God. Undo the guilt you have felt, and do the work of God. Determine your financial needs, then devote the balance to kingdom work. Please God with your prosperity.

I SURRENDER

Father, I have often sensed ingratitude and guilt over my prosperity. Help me to accept Your blessing as a gift, neither taking credit for my prosperity nor denying Your role in it. Help me use Your blessing to extend the kingdom of God here on earth. Prevent me from ever again viewing the possessions You have entrusted to me as mine. They are only a means to other ends, and I surrender them to You. Amen.

SIX

Money: The Treasure Test

"For where your treasure is, there your heart will be also."
Luke 12:34

We never do anything for only one reason. No matter what the subject, we find many desires, ambitions, and motives in our minds when we consider a particular decision.

I attend a Bible study to learn more about Christ. I am also very anxious to fit in, to be liked, and to gain the approval of the other men. We don't always consciously think about it, but we all want to be loved.

I want their approval, but I am keenly aware of human nature's frailty, so I am careful not to say anything that would damage my reputation if repeated by loose lips. And finally, I confess that I am still selfish enough to think about what someone might be able to do for me later on.

The logical question is this: If so many multiple desires, ambitions, and motives run together in our minds (and many of those subconsciously), how can we ever know if we are living a fully surrendered life, a life pleasing to God?

To Know Yourself . . .

Is there a litmus test one can take to know himself? In one sense, you cannot ever fully know yourself. "Who can discern his errors?" (Psalm 19:12). Our natural hearts always have the capacity to deceive us at any moment. Tiny pinholes in our character leak under too much pressure. And our hidden (or unknown) needs motivate us in ways we know virtually nothing about.

In another sense, though, we can walk in the power of the Holy Spirit and not gratify the desires of the sinful nature. Though dark, secret caverns dot the landscape of our minds the blood of our Savior covers, cleanses, and sanctifies the secrets of our sinful nature. "Forgive my hidden faults" (Psalm 19:12).

The Biblical Christian walks in the Spirit, while the cultural Christian gratifies the desires of the sinful nature. How can we know with certainty whether we live in the Spirit to please God, or in the flesh to please self?

Jesus knows that we are filled with a mountain of motives, an avalanche of ambitions, and a den of desires. He knows many myriad thoughts roam our minds when we make decisions. He knows that our hidden needs for approval, respect, love, and survival compel us in ways we know virtually nothing about. That's why the Scriptures indicate that deceit can so easily seep in through the pinholes of our weak character.

Even so, the question is easy to answer. The first disposition of our heart reveals whether we are a Biblical or a cultural Christian. How can we discover the first disposition of our heart?

. . . Follow the Money

Jesus said, "For where your treasure is, there your heart will be also." Jesus says how we spend our money reveals what we love, our true affections. Look at where your money went—it reveals the first disposition of your heart. Where you have stored your treasure is the record of where you have walked, either as a Biblical Christian or a cultural Christian. Follow the money.

When the government or a business suspects fraud, the auditors always follow the money. The money trail—not the verbal trail—proves what motivated the man, what the first disposition of his heart was. Although good, evil, and ambiguous motives may commingle together, where the money goes settles the record. It precisely indicates where the heart went.

If you want to know the first disposition of your heart, Jesus provides the fool-proof test. He asks, "Where is your treasure?"

Where does the money trail lead in your life? Does it please God? Have you been storing treasure like a Biblical Christian or a cultural Christian?

The cultural Christian lets "the worries of this life and the deceitfulness of wealth choke [the Word], making it unfruitful"(Matthew 13:22). The root of cultural Christianity is worry and deceit—worry over the temporary world, and deceit over what money can accomplish. To know yourself, follow the money.

If you find it difficult to segregate the multiple motives of your heart, if you find it difficult to know if you are pleasing God, then examine the record of where your treasure is. If you suspect you have lived the life of a cultural Christian, you are probably right. If you desire to please God, to be a Biblical Christian, to pass the treasure test, then redirect the trail of your money. "For where your treasure is, there will your heart be also" (Luke 12:34).

I SURRENDER

Heavenly Father, I confess that I have not been pleasing You. The record shows that I have been a cultural Christian. I want my life to please You, but I am weak and sinful. I have let the worries of this life and the deceitfulness of money choke the Word, and I have not been as fruitful as I should be. Empower me by the Spirit to make the tough choices to redirect my treasures. I surrender them to You. Do with them as You desire, according to the purpose of Your will. Amen.

SEVEN

Discipline: The Shakable Kingdom

See to it that you do not refuse him who speaks.

Hebrews 12:25

One of the great dreams is to build a business and be your own boss. As in every endeavor, there are risks as well as rewards, possible down sides as well as potential up sides.

The most common way to build a business includes debt. Debt can have personal liability or (at least in real estate) the property can often stand as sole collateral for repayment. In the early days of building our company I resisted the lure to take on personal liability. Everything we did contained a "no personal liability" clause. Then one day the irresistible deal came along. I stepped across the line. After that I signed regularly.

One morning, sometime later, I discovered a verse during my personal devotions: "Do not be a man who strikes hands in pledge or puts up security for debts; if you lack the means to pay, your very bed will be snatched from under you" (Proverbs 22:26–27).

This was not the truth I had been looking for. In fact, to follow that principle would have stopped all of my plans dead in their tracks, for I was building a real estate business and everyone knows you can't do that without mortgage debt. And much of the debt required my personal liability—meaning that *all* my assets were pledged to repay the debt, not just the asset against which the money was borrowed.

I tried everything to dilute the meaning of that verse. *Well, it's not a command, only a principle. . . . It doesn't say I will have my bed snatched, it only says if I can't pay. I will be able to pay. . . . This applies to a different time and place. Our laws don't permit losing everything—"my very bed"—the risks are different today.*

Oh, how I wished I had never seen that verse. It tortured my mind. God had spoken to me, but the best deals all seemed to require personal liability. I had a clear choice to make: My plans or the Word of God. Build the business based on mortgage debt which required personal guarantees; or change my plans, go slowly, and refuse to strike my hand in pledge.

"See to it that you do not refuse him who speaks." (Hebrews 12:25) Do not cross His line. The problem with crossing the line—refusing Him who speaks—is that once you have done it, each successive temptation to cross it again becomes easier and easier. Finally, your dulled senses no longer even distinguish that you are refusing Him who speaks. What is the line He has shown you? Have you stepped across it yet? "Do not refuse Him who speaks."

THE CONSEQUENCES

What is the destiny of the person who refuses Him who speaks?

If they did not escape when they refused him who warned them on earth, how much less will we, if we turn away from him who warns us from heaven? At that time his voice shook the earth, but now he has promised, "Once more I will shake not only the earth but also the heavens." The words "once more" indicate the removing of what can be shaken—that is, created things—so that what cannot be shaken may remain (Hebrews 12:25–27).

God declares that He will faithfully remove the created things which can be shaken—the shakable kingdom. Why? So that the unshakable may remain. Created things which give cultural Christianity its toe-hold. It is created things that defeat us and choke the Word—"the worries of this life and the deceitfulness of wealth" (Matthew 13:22).

When we cross over the line and refuse Him who speaks, He will separate us from the created things—the idols, the shakable kingdom—which dilute our devotion to Him. If we cannot remain obedient, if we cannot be holy, then He will discipline us for our own good, "that we may share in his holiness."

If God is removing or has removed the created things—the shakable—then be glad. For when the shakable is removed, the unshakable remains. The removal of created things is a blessing. The right response to cultural Christianity's removal is gratitude: "Therefore, since we are receiving a kingdom which cannot be shaken, let us be thankful" (Hebrews 12:28).

IT HAPPENS TO THE NICEST PEOPLE

Do not be alarmed if God shakes up your world. Though your first natural thought will disagree, it is a blessing. It is not a sign that you are unworthy—every one of us is unworthy. It is not a sign of hatred, but love. If He did not love you, He would let you completely self-destruct. As it is, He cleanses your life from sin. "Some of the wise will stumble, so that they may be refined, purified and made spotless until the time of the end, for it will still come at the appointed time" (Daniel 11:35).

When God disciplines you by removing created things, by shaking up your temporal kingdom, rejoice and be glad. Created things divide our affections from God and become competition to our devotion. They lure us into the wrong race. They consume our creativity and deflect our thoughts away from the Lord Jesus.

I became a cultural Christian. Created things became idols and divided me from complete, faithful devotion to our Lord. God removed most of the created things I accumulated. I had built a shakable kingdom, and God shook it. Words are inadequate to express the joy and gratitude I feel toward God for the wounds He faithfully inflicted. It may be the single greatest blessing of my spiritual pilgrimage.

The removal of the shakable gave me a deep respect and awe for the character of God, especially His holiness. Gone was the folly that I could outmaneuver God. "Be thankful, and so worship God acceptably with reverence and awe, for our 'God is a consuming fire'" (Hebrews 12:28–29). He is jealous to the point of removing created things.

GOD NEVER OVER-DISCIPLINES

When my children refuse me when I speak my normal tendency is to over-react. If my daughter deserves to be sent to her room for one hour, I tend to send her for two. I over-discipline.

God never over-disciplines. You can trust God. When He shakes the shakable, when He removes the removable, He is perfect in His discipline of us. In fact, because of His great mercy we can often join Ezra and say, "You have punished us less than our sins have deserved" (Ezra 9:13). Sometimes God under-disciplines.

When God lovingly inflicts pain and removes the shakable, know that you are blessed. He is purging the cultural Christianity from your life. He is making you holy even as He is holy. "Endure hardship as discipline" (Hebrews 12:7).

I SURRENDER

My God and Father, how I have longed to know why You have shaken my life. Now I must confess that I have been building a shakable kingdom. You are making me holy. How I thank You, dear Lord, for Your faithfulness to remove the created things which have divided me from loving You with all of my heart, soul, mind, and strength. I surrender the temporal kingdom I have been building to You, and ask You to show me how to worship You acceptably with reverence and awe. Amen.

EIGHT

Materialism: Divided Interests

Those who buy something, [should live] as if it were not theirs to keep; those who use the things of the world, as if not engrossed in them.

1 Corinthians 7:30–31

Webster's Dictionary defines *materialism* as, "The theory that physical well-being and worldly possessions constitute the highest value and greatest good in life." Is that true? Do comfort and belongings mark what's most important to us? Of course not. Yet we must confess that, although we wish it weren't true, our lives often reveal that material has hold of us.

Two things occur when we reflect on this. First, we see ourselves all too clearly. Second, the Word commands us not to let the blemishes of the world stain our soul. Why? "For this world in its present form is passing away" (1 Corinthians 7:31). God wants us to live for the world that is coming, not for the world that is going.

I can recall so vividly the days of my unbridled materialism. I wanted to be a Biblical Christian, but I was so engrossed in my own worldly affairs that I simply did not penetrate the spiritual life deeply, even though I sincerely wanted to. Do you see the trap? We can congratulate ourselves for our *good intentions* while continuing to live a secular lifestyle, believing intentions are as good as actions.

Truth be known, many of us live more for the world that is going than the world that is coming. It takes time, lots of time, to manage all the "things" we accumulate. Time, in the final analysis, is the ultimate resource. It is even how we get our money. Where are you spending your time? Pleasing God, or managing your assets? The Lord says, "I would like you to be free from concern," (1 Corinthians 7:32). Is that the record of our calendar and checkbook?

Only a unique person could climb the corporate ladder all day, be absorbed in worldly affairs, and then slow down to the pace of Jesus. Here's the problem: We all tend to think we are that unique person. We are the one who can do it; we are unique, we can manage to maximize two worlds. We cannot.

We can only maximize one world. We will be engrossed in the affairs of this world or we will be engrossed in how to please the Lord. "*No one* can serve two masters" (Matthew 6:24, emphasis added). Do you see it? According to the Word of God, *there are no unique people*. No one can pull it off, but we always think we can. It is time for some of us to confront our own materialism. Have you been trying to maximize two worlds? Have you tried to serve two masters?

The action plan is hard. It is simple, but hard. You must surrender all the things you have bought and every worldly thing you are using to the Lord. "Those who buy something, as if it were not theirs to keep; those who use the things of the world, as if not engrossed in them."

He may let you keep some or all of your things; He may increase them. Or He may prune you back to a useful level. If you listen to His leading He will clarify His desire for you. If you don't listen, He will gain your attention in other ways. He works in our lives regardless of our level of cooperation, but surrender produces the most fruit.

We must adjust our lifestyles until they offer a viable alternative—an alternative of hope—to the confused and broken world all around us, a world that is passing away. Give what you don't need to the work of Christ. Devote time to loving one another. And remember that the time is short. Live for the world that is coming, not for the world that is going. "For this world in its present form is passing away" (1 Corinthians 7:31).

I SURRENDER

Heavenly Father, I confess that too much of my life has been spent on comfort and belongings. Show me how to maximize my spiritual life. Give me the courage to recant my materialism. I want my lifestyle to speak for itself. Help me to live for the world that is coming, and not for the world that is going. Amen.

NINE

Surrender: A Recovering Materialist

Death and Destruction are never satisfied, and neither are the eyes of man.

Proverbs 27:20

At the moment of my conversion to faith in Christ, my two-pronged life philosophy was moralism and material-ism. There was nothing happenchance about this philos-ophy; it represented years of searching for purpose and meaning. I wanted to become financially independent, as well as to do the right thing by each person I met. It felt right, for awhile.

The life philosophy of a moral materialist (or a mate-rial moralist) turned out not to be enough. I sensed I didn't have a purpose big enough to last a lifetime.

When the Father drew me toward Jesus, I "added" Christ to my life. In other words, I didn't stop being a moralist and a materialist. Rather, I added Christ to my existing life philosophy, I suppose with the notion that Christ could fill in the missing pieces which caused my lack of purpose.

For the first decade of my spiritual life I was a moralist and a materialistic and a Christian. To be a moralist and a Christian is no compromise. In fact, it is a good thing to have already settled that issue before receiving God's grace. But to be a materialist is a profound contradiction with Christianity. Materialism, "the theory that physical well-being and worldly possessions constitute the highest value and greatest good in life," is the *exact* opposite of Christianity. Yet, materialism is the predominant value of the world.

So how can one be a materialist and a Christian? One cannot. It is a theoretical, rational, and empirical impossibility. It is like trying to mix oil and water.

Now, there is no doubt that my conversion was real and that I became a Christian. So how is it that I continued to live the life of a materialist? How can anyone continue to live the life of a materialist? When we are truly converted we (by definition) no longer subscribe to the tenets of materialism. We are disciples of Jesus and not materialism, yet we still wrestle with being materialistic, "one relating to or marked by materialism." The distinction is between adding Christ to our lives versus surrendering to Him.

When we settle on being a "materialistic" Christian we are trying to have the best of both worlds—the kingdom of God and the world which is passing away. Our eyes are never satisfied; contentment eludes us; we become cultural Christians. Little marginal difference distinguishes between our lifestyle and the lifestyle of the broken, hurting world around us. So what should we do about it?

When I became convicted of the materialism of my life, I wanted to change—but not more than I wanted to stay the same, because nothing happened. Yet over a period of several years God, in His tender, loving way, slowly removed the scales from my eyes. He showed me both convicting and faith-building Scriptures on the subject. He disciplined me, I persevered, my character grew, and the hope that I could change finally took root. One day, when my spirit had been fortified, I plunged into a commitment to give up materialism altogether. I prayed, "Give me neither poverty nor riches."

Today I am a recovering materialist. I am quite certain that once someone is a materialist, he is always a materialist. "Death and Destruction are never satisfied, and neither are the eyes of man" (Proverbs 27:20). It is a disease, like alcoholism or gambling. And, as once an alcoholic always an alcoholic, I am quite certain that once you are a materialist you are always a materialist.

Does this mean that if you are pursuing materialism that you are not a Christian? No, not if you have received Him as Savior and Lord. But it does mean that over a lifetime you will reap judgment if you live by the values of the world and not of God. "A man reaps what he sows" (Galatians 6:7). Materialism is sin. Possessions are not sin, but an obsession for possessions is.

Guard your heart against materialism. It is born of the sinful nature. "The one who sows to please his sinful nature, from that nature will reap destruction; the one who sows to please the Spirit, from the Spirit will reap eternal life" (Galatians 6:8). If you continue to live for money you are like a gambler who vacations in Las Vegas or an alcoholic who takes work in a brewery. Are your eyes never satisfied? How far have you wandered? Is it time to become a "recovering" materialist?

I SURRENDER

Lord Jesus, I confess that I have been trying to have the best of both worlds. I am a materialist. I am piercing myself with many griefs: overwork, debt, broken relationships, and stress. Forgive me for trying to serve both God and Money. When I first believed, I "added" You to my life. Now I want to surrender to You. Grant me the grace, I pray, to want neither poverty nor riches. In Your mercy, allow me to become a recovering materialist. Amen.

TEN

Failure: A Six-Point Formula for Spiritual Failure

... so that you may be able to discern what is best and may be pure and blameless until the day of Christ.

Philippians 1:10

Do you ever have that vague, inarticulate sense that even though you are a Christian, you have gotten yourself turned around and may be living by the wrong set of motives, ambitions, and priorities?

Ed served as an elder in his church, tithed, and gave his whole life to the work of God. Yet, after twenty years of Christian life, he became embittered toward God, and walked away. What should make each of us shudder is the frequency with which this scenario repeats itself. We all know people who have become embittered and walked away. Why does it happen? And what can we each do to inoculate ourselves from the disease of terminal spiritual bitterness?

Sometimes our lives can get so turned around that we think, *I feel like chucking the whole thing*. These are the moments of spiritual disillusionment. How do we become spiritually disillusioned? Let's take a look at how to do things wrong.

Here is a six-step, fool-proof formula for spiritual failure. Look for yourself in these six steps and perform some self-diagnosis.

1. *Go with the Natural Flow of Life.* To be a successful failure requires that you not give much thought to knowing Jesus more intimately on a day-to-day basis. Think of Him more as a distant relative than a close friend. Let life's natural currents take you where they may. Don't look for a spiritual rhythm and tempo to daily life. Presume that spiritual growth will occur naturally. Don't expend too much time in reflection, examining life's larger purpose and meaning. It will give you a headache.

2. *Immerse Yourself in Christian Work.* One of the great secrets to finding spiritual disillusionment is to give yourself fully to the busyness of Christian life. Be there every time the church doors open. Cook the pancakes, balance the budget, call on all the first-time visitors. Spend your time doing the work of God, and don't bog down in the Scriptures and intercession for the saints. It's okay not to know your spiritual gifts because you can employ your natural abilities for service. Let your credo be, "To serve Him is to know Him."

3. *Do More for God Each Year.* Measure your value to God by results. Keep records of your spiritual production. If you spent one hundred hours in Christian service last year, then make one hundred twenty hours your goal for this year. Make performance the acid test of your spirituality. Don't listen to idle chatter that faithfulness is more important that production. Be American—let performance be your standard.

4. *Look for Feedback from Friends.* Measure your spiritual value by the feedback you get from other people. Depend on the appreciation and affirmation of the brothers and sisters. Savor the comments of your friends; turn them over and over in your mind. Believe what they say. Let their strokes provide energy, strength, and encouragement. Gain your identity in your accomplishments. Derive your self-worth from how others value your achievements, possibly in commerce, but especially in ministry.

5. *Build a Reputation.* Pick service to God that is high visibility. Build a spiritual ministry. Gain a reputation. Don't be satisfied being a servant; become a star. If you can become somebody important, you can make a bigger contribution. Don't think much about doing service for the glory of God. He can manage His own glory. Do your service in such a way that you are noticed. This is an excellent way to advance to bigger and better opportunities to serve God.

6. *Concentrate on Work That Helps People.* People really are very needy, you know, and if you position yourself correctly you can become like a mini-Mother Teresa. Keep telling yourself that working for the betterment of mankind is worth it—it is a worthwhile goal in and of itself. Convince yourself that you will leave the world a better place. Believe that the issue on Christ's mind is easing the pain of life alone, not seeking and saving lost sinners. Don't focus on the distinction between showing human sympathy and confronting lost sinners with the loving claims of the gospel.

The other way—the way to spiritual success—is the opposite of what the world would prescribe.

With Christ, success is not performance; it's surrender. To succeed is to surrender your motives, ambitions, and priorities to Christ. Seek to know Him more personally. Measure your worth and gain your identity by faithfulness to Christ, not by production. Let your service come from the overflow of a vital daily communion with the living Lord.

I Surrender

Lord, sometimes I do feel like chucking the whole thing. I am concerned that I'm on a collision course with spiritual disillusionment and bitterness. I often apply secular methods to meeting spiritual needs. I see myself in some of these six areas. Where I am walking the path to disillusionment I pray You will redirect my steps. I confess I have been living by a confused set of motives, ambitions, and priorities. I surrender them to you. Amen.

ELEVEN

Resurrender: The Way Back

"Here I am! I stand at the door and knock. If anyone
hears my voice and opens the door, I will come in and
eat with him, and he with me."

Revelation 3:20

When I speak at an evangelistic outreach meeting (like a prayer breakfast or luncheon), I always mention that Revelation 3:20 is my favorite verse in the Bible. Let me tell you why.

In the past I closed evangelistic meetings by offering the audience the opportunity to express faith and receive Christ by silently praying a sinner's prayer. In recent times, though, I close with two prayers—one for those God is calling that day (see John 6:44), and another for those who have not been walking with the Lord and long to find their way back.

For the second prayer I make it very clear and very precise that I am referring specifically to those men and women who have once known the joy of receiving Christ but are not in fellowship with Him. They have taken control of their lives. They have pursued the God they wanted instead of the God who is. They are not walking with Christ. They are cultural Christians and not Biblical Christians.

Why would I approach Christians with the Gospel in this way? In my experience, nearly everyone has "prayed a prayer," especially in the South. America has been saturated with the Gospel, and countless millions have leaped at the chance to receive Christ without knowing or counting the cost.

Many of these people leave the revival meetings and go about the business of life as usual. They don't obey Christ, meditate on the Word, talk with God, or manifest the changed life of those who had surrendered their will to almighty God.

When one prayer to receive Christ and a second to resurrender to Him are both offered, those who resurrender always outnumber the first-time decisions. I think it's great! Dwight L. Moody once said, "I would rather wake up a slumbering church than a slumbering world."

I offer the Revelation 3:20 passage as the way back for broken Christians. In that verse Christ speaks to the *church* at Laodicea. They were a lot like us. They became prosperous and self-reliant. The Lord addressed them this way: "You say, 'I am rich; I have acquired wealth and do not need a thing'" (Revelation 3:17).

Jesus sternly warned the Laodiceans. "'I know your deeds, that you are neither cold nor hot. I wish you were either one or the other! So, because you are lukewarm—neither hot nor cold—I am about to spit you out of my mouth'" (Revelation 3:15–16).

We live in a profoundly religious country, and we are a prosperous people. But we are also a broken people—a people who have pursued the God of our own imaginations, believing we can re-create His character to suit our own practical problems. The result? We are the most religious nation in the world but, like the Laodiceans, many are lukewarm.

Prosperous Christians become lukewarm. Lukewarm Christians rely upon themselves, they forget the terms of their surrender to Christ. Instead of living by the will of God they live according to the self-will, and fellowship with God is broken. We live in a broken generation.

In Revelation 3:20 Jesus offers to reestablish fellowship with broken, lukewarm, cultural Christians. He cries out His warning and His offer to the church. Long before the idea struck Moody, Jesus spoke to wake up a slumbering church. He said, "'Those whom I love I rebuke and discipline. So be earnest, and repent. Here I am! I stand at the door and knock. If anyone hears my voice and opens the door, I will come in and eat with him, and he with me'" (Revelation 3:19–20).

He is the way back. When we become complacent, when we stop walking with Him, He still loves us. He despises our behavior, but He wants to restore fellowship with us.

DINING WITH GOD

A quiet dinner with friends in their home epitomizes fellowship. The door bell rings. The door swings wide. Eyes meet. Smiles erupt on happy faces. Friends embrace. The hosts invite their dear friends in.

The warm, encouraging conversation that flows easily over the table over a fondly prepared feast symbolizes the high-water mark of fellowship. Christ picked this very symbol to express what happens when we repent and open the door of our heart and resurrender to Him. "'I will come in and eat with him, and he with me'" (v.20).

Have you been lukewarm? Have you thought to yourself, *I have acquired wealth and do not need a thing?* If so, Jesus is standing at the door, knocking. Jesus is gentle and quiet, and He never forces Himself into our lives. Instead, He knocks and softly whispers His offer. Do you hear it? It is my favorite. For those who are not walking with Him, it is the way back. "'Here I am! I stand at the door [of your life] and knock. If anyone hears my voice and opens the door, I will come in. . . .'" (v.20).

If you have not been walking with the Lord and long to find the way back, invite Him in. If the following prayer expresses the desire of your heart, then pray it, and dine with the living Christ.

I SURRENDER

Lord Jesus, though I haven't thought much about it, I have acted as though I have acquired wealth and do not need a thing. I have become luke-warm, and I have not been walking with You as I should. I long to restore fellowship with You, the living Lord. I confess that I have been more of a cultural Christian than a Biblical Christian. I repent of my self-seeking, self-reliant ways. I open the door of my life and resurrender my will to You. Take control of my life and make me into the kind of person You want me to be. Thank You for coming in. Amen.

TWELVE

Values: Making a Comeback

> *See to it that no one takes you captive through hollow*
> *and deceptive philosophy, which depends on human*
> *tradition and the basic principles of this world rather*
> *than on Christ.*
>
> Colossians 2:8

For several years John met with a small group of men. They experienced a real bond in Christ—a heart-tie— and they were mutually committed to the Lord. They met regularly for Bible Study and accountability. There was nothing superficial in their relationships.

Some of the brothers in his group counseled John against becoming involved in a questionable business relationship, but John forged ahead anyway. Soon, his desire to come apart daily to meet with the Lord diminished. He eventually dropped out of the group. Several years later his values only vaguely reflected Biblical principles. Over a span of several years a swirling whirlpool of selfish desires relentlessly pulled him into its vortex until, one day, the world finally swallowed him up, just as Jonah was swallowed into the belly of a great fish. He walked away from God.

Are you at high risk to be swallowed up? Once someone walks away from the Lord it is hard to make a comeback. It is easier to continue in Christ than to make a comeback. "So then, just as you received Christ Jesus as Lord, *continue to live in him*, rooted and built up in him" (Colossians 2:6, emphasis added).

What poses the greatest risk to not continuing in Christ? The greatest risk is the *crisis of values* which inexorably comes when we follow hollow and deceptive philosophy. It may not come until we have traveled for many years down the road of self-deceit, but it will come.

The crisis of values is no less than a bad case of the *-ism's*—materialism, relativism, humanism, hedonism, liberalism, secularism and so on. I doubt few of us ever set out to become a materialist or a relativist or whatever. It is more that without self-examination we atrophy from the Christian value system into something less. Not that we abandon the spiritual tie, but that slowly, almost imperceptibly, we undo the moral knot to which we pledged ourselves. When once we redraw the line, there is less pressure against redrawing it again, and less and less each time thereafter.

WHY COMEBACKS ARE HARD

The reason it is harder to make a comeback than to continue in Christ has to do with God. We have to deal with the effects of sin in our lives. Once we have undergone and completed His discipline, He rejoices and welcomes us with celebration. But the road back is a hard road. We have left a trail of casualties: hurt people, broken relationships, poor choices, consequences, financial problems, and lots of pain—emotional and spiritual pain.

God wants us to make a comeback. He wants us to make a comeback more than we do. Nothing frustrates an employer more than to want an employee to succeed more than the employee himself wants to succeed. God is the same; He wants us to succeed. This is transparent, because were it not for His grace none of us would ever be able to make the comeback. He finds us; we don't find Him.

HOW TO START A COMEBACK

How can someone start a comeback? From the belly of the great fish Jonah cried out, "When my life was ebbing away, I remembered you, Lord, and my prayer rose to you, to your holy temple. Those who cling to worthless idols [the *-ism's*] forfeit the grace that could be theirs" (Jonah 2:7–8). Jonah could not know it, but when he humbled himself, God initiated his comeback. When we humble ourselves and turn back, God initiates our comeback.

At the point Jonah turned back, how did God respond? Did He call for a celebration? No, He did not. Once we have been swallowed up, the first step back is merely to make it back to dry land. "And the Lord commanded the fish, and it vomited Jonah onto dry land" (Jonah 2:10).

When we start on the comeback we start from where we have been—in the belly of the world which swallowed us up. God spits us up onto the shore by His grace, it is an inauspicious starting point from which to make a comeback.

The comeback will be embarrassing. The odor of where we have been remains until we cleanse ourselves. The people we hurt will not trust us at first. We must still work through the human consequences of having untied the moral knot—of being taken captive by hollow and deceptive philosophy. Painful and embarrassing it may be, but He does let us come back.

Do you have a case of the *-ism's*? Have you been taken captive, swallowed up into the belly of the world? If you have been swallowed up, are you ready yet to humble yourself? Are you ready to start your comeback? If you are willing, He is willing.

I SURRENDER

Lord, I have been swallowed up by the world. I have a case of the *-ism's*. Lord, my life was ebbing away, but I have remembered You. Do not let me forfeit Your grace. Grant me a second chance. I renounce the idols and *-ism's* which have slowly swallowed me up. Help me retie the moral knot. Help me to make a comeback. Amen.

THIRTEEN

Dependency: The Safety of the Unmet Need

The widow who is really in need and left all alone puts her hope in God and continues night and day to pray and to ask God for help.

1 Timothy 5:5

Several men went on a mission trip to Haiti where they met a nineteen-year-old Haitian boy who loved Christ deeply. He impressed them so profoundly that they invited him to visit the United States.

Upon arrival a whole new world opened up before this young Haitian's eyes. He had never slept between sheets, never had three meals all on the same day, never used indoor plumbing, and never tasted McDonald's. Back in Haiti he lived in a mud hut.

While traveling the U.S., this godly young man made many new friends. At the end of a six-weeks-long visit, his sponsors hosted a farewell dinner in his honor. After dinner several members of the group offered warm parting remarks with voices that cracked. Then they asked the young Haitian if he would like to say anything.

"Yes," he said as he rose, "I would. I want to thank you so much for inviting me here. I have really enjoyed this time in the United States. But I am also very glad to be going home. You have so much in America, that I'm beginning to lose my grip on my day-to-day dependency on Christ."

Do you have "so much" that you find it hard to keep a grip on your day-to-day dependency on Christ? Or worse, have you lost your grip?

When we have "so much" that we don't need to depend on Christ, we will not. It is part—maybe even a curse—of human nature. Our natural tendency is to depend on self, not Christ. Depending on Christ is an act of the will by faith, not the natural disposition of our heart.

THE PRAYER FOR AN UNMET NEED

I have prayed that God will always keep some major unmet need in my life so that I will always depend upon Him. To be "really in need," like the widow in 1 Timothy 5:5, creates dependency. To have "so much," as the young Haitian observed, creates self-sufficiency. When our lives prosper, the natural tendency is to lose our grip.

Someone called my prayer courageous. I disagree. It is not a prayer of courage, but of fear—the fear of a holy God. For God has the power to give us what we deserve, whether good or bad. I have come to fear, with reverence and awe, the God who is, for He is a consuming fire.

The Scriptures teach that "the widow who is *really* in need . . . puts her hope in God and continues night and day to pray and ask God for help" (v.5). Are you in need? Do you put your hope in God? Do you continue to pray night and day and ask God for help? Or do you have so much that you don't need to depend on Christ for the details of your life?

If you have lost—or are losing—your grip on your day-to-day dependency on Christ, ask God for an unmet need. When you are "really in need," you will put all your hope in God, not your own ability. You will pray night and day and ask God for help, you will not depend on your own resources. You will *use* your ability and resources, but you will *depend* on Christ.

A friend of mine frequently says, "You will never know Jesus is all you need until Jesus is all you have." God loves people who depend upon Him, people who stop pursuing the God they want and surrender to the God who is.

First Timothy 5:6 continues, "But the widow who lives for pleasure is dead even while she lives." Is your faith in Christ dead or alive? When we live for pleasure we lose our grip. When "so much" gets in the way of our day-to-day dependency on Christ, we grieve the Holy Spirit.

Ask God to make you more like the widow who put her hope in God alone and continues to pray and ask God for help. That is day-to-day dependency on Christ. If you do this, you will never lose your grip. She depended on God because she was "really in need." There is safety in an unmet need. That's not courageous; that's just smart.

I SURRENDER

Dear Father, I must admit I have "so much" that it is hard for me to maintain a good grip on my day-to-day dependency on Christ. Let me know the blessing and joy of being really in need so that I may put my hope in You alone and not my own ability and resources. Work in me to desire to pray night and day and ask You for help. How I long to know the God who really is. I want to be different than I have been. I want to be a Biblical Christian. By faith I make a full, total, complete, no-reserves, no-regrets surrender of my life to You. Amen.

FOURTEEN

The Fear of the Lord: Love Wisdom and Hate Evil

The fear of the Lord leads to life: Then one rests content, untouched by trouble.

Proverbs 19:23

Are you content? Is your life untouched by trouble? Learn to understand the fear of the Lord.

About ten years ago I attended a Christian wedding for which the bride and groom wrote their own wedding vows. As the solemn, joyful moment came, they faced each other, clasped hands, and exchanged those vows.

The bride said, "And the reason I love you and want to spend my life with you is that you understand the fear of the Lord." What is the fear of the Lord? Do you understand it? Is it important to you?

Many of us have lost the fear of the Lord. We have forgotten our deep awe for the character of God, His holiness, His eternality, His sovereignty over all the affairs of men. We let Him get smaller. We let our impression of ourselves get bigger. We see ourselves as larger in intellect and capabilities, as more technologically advanced and more scientific. As we prosper we don't need God as we once did.

What is the fear of the Lord? And how can we get it into our lives? The fear of the Lord is to love what God loves and to hate what God hates. The fear of the Lord has a positive and a negative.

LOVE WISDOM

The positive is to love what God loves—wisdom. God loves wisdom. The fear of the Lord is to love wisdom. "My son, if you accept my words and store up my commands within you, turning your ear to wisdom and applying your heart to understanding ... then you will understand the fear of the Lord and find the knowledge of God. For the Lord gives wisdom" (Proverbs 2:1–2, 5–6).

To love wisdom is to fear the Lord. "'The fear of the Lord—that is wisdom'" (Job 28:28). The person who would understand the fear of the Lord will love what God loves. God loves wisdom, so he will love wisdom.

Wisdom comes from God alone. Many want to add their own unique theories to the wisdom of God. We often want new ideas, new truth. But the pages of Holy Writ give testimony to the durability of God's wisdom over man's fresh ideas.

When we add to the wisdom of God, it does not become the wisdom of God plus something, but the wisdom of God minus something. Can we lead a rebellion against the eternal God? Can we be His teacher? Let us learn to love the wisdom of God, then we will understand the fear of the Lord.

HATE EVIL

The negative is to hate what God hates—evil. God hates evil. "To fear the Lord is to hate evil" (Proverbs 8:13).

"Through the fear of the Lord a man avoids evil" (Proverbs 16:6). "To shun evil is understanding" (Job 28:28). The person who would understand the fear of the Lord will hate what God hates. God hates evil, so he will hate evil.

What differentiates the person who understands the fear of the Lord from the one who does not? The person not gripped by the fear of God tolerates evil. He does not take exception to the moral filth which permeates culture. He doesn't like it, but his motto is, "Live and let live." He is not *of* the world, but neither is he *into* the world. He is God's person *in* the world, but not been sent *into* the world. He has no impact, because he tolerates evil.

The person gripped by godly fear cannot tolerate evil because God does not tolerate evil. He hates evil with the intensity that God hates evil, or at least he tries to. He is a reformer, not a recluse. His hatred of evil sanctions him no occasion to tolerate.

TWO IN ONE

The fear of the Lord consists both in loving and hating. It is loving what God loves—wisdom, and hating what God hates—evil. When we love what God loves and hate what He hates, we are not far from the kingdom of God. "The fear of the Lord leads to life: Then one rests content, untouched by trouble"(Proverbs 19:23). Do you know what God loves? Do you know what God hates?

THE ANTIDOTE FOR DISOBEDIENCE

How important is this ignored injunction to fear the Lord? Solomon waxed eloquent for twelve chapters in Ecclesiastes about the futility of pursuing temporal kingdoms. At the end of the book, he summarized: "Now all has been heard; here is the conclusion of the matter: Fear God and keep his commandments, for this is the whole duty of man" (Ecclesiastes 12:13). Though we have lost the fear of the Lord, our duty is to find it again.

The fear of the Lord is the antidote for disobedience. The Hebrew people pledged obedience to God when Moses declared the ten commandments to them. God responded to their pledge: "Oh, that their hearts would be inclined to fear me and keep my commandments always" (Deuteronomy 5:29). God links obedience to the fear of the Lord—it is the antidote for disobedience.

I SURRENDER

Father, teach me the fear of the Lord. I surrender my own clever ideas that I would add to Your wisdom. Help me to love what You love—wisdom. Help me to hate what you hate—evil. Take away my tolerance of evil that I might be a reformer, that I might be sent "into" the world and not merely take up space "in" the world. Amen.

PART THREE

Our Relationship with Christ

The turning point of our lives is when we stop seeking the God we want, and start seeking the God who is.

FIFTEEN

Jesus: Commitment to a Person Versus a Set of Values

"Follow me."

Matthew 9:9

While we were still dating, I convinced Patsy—now wife, then fiancée—that I was a Christian. Shortly after our wedding it became obvious that we had an ambiguity of terms over what it meant to be Christian. I was committed to a set of Christian *values*, but I learned she was committed to a *Person*.

One can be committed to Christian values but still not be a Christian, as I soon found out. To be committed to a set of Christian values is to be a *moralist*, but not necessarily a *Christian*. The commitment is to be a "good" person to the best of one's ability.

The inevitable result of committing to a set of Christian values is disillusionment and confusion. We are not good. We may not be as bad as we could possibly be, but neither are we as good as God expects. No one can live a moral life in their own power, so we renegotiate our values down over time. We settle for a compromised level of integrity.

Through the clouded eyes of self-deceit, we lose sight of the pervasiveness of our sins. We may feel envy toward our friends, have a secret thought life of fantasy, or explode in fits of anger more painful to our family than physical blows. We make ourselves feel better by comparing ourselves to the "national average" instead of the standard of the Living Word.

WHAT'S THE DIFFERENCE?

What difference does it make whether we are committed to a set of values or a Person? It is not the *way* of Christ that leads to everlasting life; it is the *Person* of Christ. It is trusting Him to produce the spiritual life in us, not trusting in ourselves to produce the spiritual life by our own effort.

I could not understand this difference at first. It was not transparent to me. The distinction seemed inconsequential. Yet, as I learned more and more, the difference began to come into focus. It is a huge distinction. For those who want to know God, it is the dividing line. Do you know it?

Jesus says simply, "Follow me." When we are weary and burdened Jesus gives us rest—not our values. He says, "Follow *me*," He does not say "Follow my *principles*." It is His life that connects us to God, not emulating His "goodness." If we imitate His life but don't know Him personally, we will become exhausted. We can see that which is good, right, and pure, but we do not have the *power* to live up to it. Only Christ in you can live up to it.

How do we become committed to the Person of Christ? We must by faith allow our "self" to be crucified with Christ so that His power may be released within us, the power of the Holy Spirit. "I have been crucified with Christ and I no longer live, but Christ lives in me. The life I live in the body, I live by faith in the Son of God, who loved me and gave himself for me" (Galatians 2:20). It is a Person who lives in me, not a set of values. We don't invite a set of values to indwell us; we invite the Spirit of the living Christ.

IMITATION VERSUS SURRENDER

Today church pews are bloated with well-meaning people—people who sincerely want to be Christian. But they are confused. They believe (and their church often confirms) that the Christian life is a commitment to a set of values. Who would question such a noble thought? Jesus would. He said, "I am the way. No one come to the Father except through me" (John 14:6). Not through values.

It is not imitation that leads to everlasting life; it is surrender. It is not guessing what Christ would do and imitating Him; it is acknowledging we cannot imitate Him at all. It is accepting that His blood was spilled on the cross because we cannot imitate Him. It is to surrender our will, heart, mind, soul, and strength to the Person who died for us.

It is not *what* we follow, but *who* we follow; not a set of values but a Person. It is not "the life I live in the body, I live by these *values*." It is "the life I live in the body, I live by *faith*." Faith is confidence in the Person of Christ and the atoning work He did through the shedding of His blood for our sins, not in the merit of living up to a set of values.

Well-meaning people come to the foot of the cross to be refreshed. They are deeply encouraged that they don't have to *do* something to become Christian, only that they must admit they *cannot* do anything apart from the Master. But as they go on their way, they can "see" the values of Jesus, while He Himself remains invisible, enigmatic, mysterious. It is easier to follow what is seen than what is unseen, so people gravitate to living by a set of values. It is not faith in Christ.

Well-meaning people often begin their pilgrimage committed to His Person, but later place their faith in what they do for Him (the seen) instead of what He has done for them (the unseen). But, "We live by faith, not by sight" (2 Corinthians 5:7). If you live by sight you will lose the joy of your salvation.

Are you committed to a set of Christian values or are you committed to a Person for your salvation? If you began your pilgrimage by receiving Christ, are you still living by faith, or has your confidence returned to a set of values?

I SURRENDER

Lord Jesus, I must admit that I often become more committed to a set of Christian values than to You. I have not spent the time getting to know You that I should. I have failed to answer Your call, "Follow me." Instead, I have been following my own good idea of what it would mean to be a Christian. I have wanted to be a good person, but I now see that You want me to trust only You for my spiritual destiny and not my own effort. Forgive my sins, take control of my life, and make me into a follower of You—not the follower of a set of values. Amen.

SIXTEEN

Christ: Is There Another?

"Lord, to whom shall we go?"
John 6:68

For more than a dozen years I have met weekly with a man for fellowship, prayer, and accountability. For the first several years the relationship passed through several veneers. Each time we peeled back another layer and became more transparent and vulnerable, the relationship leaped to a higher (or deeper) level. The culminating stage is a simple acceptance of each other.

Through the years each of us have agonized through our fair share of grueling problems and trials. We have often said to each other, "The Christian life is a hard life." The other nods in knowing agreement. A short "woe is me" speech usually follows.

Then, as we commiserate, we always come around to the same supreme question, "Where else would you go? If there were a better way, I would choose it. But as hard as it is, Christ is the best answer."

In the weakest moment of our faith, in the darkest hour of doubt, we turn back to Jesus. Why? "'Lord, to whom shall we go? You have the words of eternal life'"

(John 6:68). Hard as life is, without Jesus it is no life at all, but death and despair.

Here is the idea to get hold of: The only reason we don't desert Him in our weak moment is because of His commitment to us, not because of our commitment to Him. "'Have I not chosen you?'" (John 6:70).

We don't turn back to Him. Though embarrassing to admit, if we could find a better way, we would. When we find out He is not the God we wanted, we are sorely disappointed. His teachings are hard (see John 6:60). He won't give us what we want. He won't work the way we want Him to work. "From this time many of his disciples turned back and no longer followed him" (John 6:66).

The best way is this: I will change. I will want Him and Him alone. I know that there is no better way (for I have tried and failed with so many false gods). And I accept that the reason I know He is the only way is because He chose me, not because I chose Him.

I Surrender

Lord Jesus, I will not resist You. I have told You about all the things I want from You. Now tell me what You want from me. Thank You for choosing me. I know that if it was not for Your love for me I would never have found You. In my darkest hours I have thought of leaving, but to whom would I go? Amen.

SEVENTEEN

Born Again: The Dramatic Conversion

Jesus declared, "I tell you the truth, no one can see the kingdom of God unless he is born again."

John 3:3

There is no equivocation by Jesus on this matter of new birth. But some Christians suffer a deep misunderstanding of what it actually means to be "born again."

A Christian friend argued vehemently that he was *not* born again, though he was equally vociferous that he had received Jesus Christ as his personal Lord and Savior. How could that be? Actually, it cannot be. Christ left no margin for dispute: "'I tell you the truth, unless a man is born of water and the Spirit, he cannot enter the kingdom of God. Flesh gives birth to flesh, but the Spirit gives birth to spirit'" (John 3:5–6).

The main point of confusion boils down to the issue of the dramatic conversion. The greatest stories of men receiving Christ are often the most dramatic ones. The appearance of Jesus in blinding light terrified Saul during his dramatic conversion on the Damascus road. Martin

Luther, a brilliant young sixteenth-century legal mind, dodged a lightning bolt, committed his life to the ministry, and fathered the Protestant Reformation.

The misunderstanding arises from putting an equal sign between *dramatic conversion* and *born again*. They are different issues. *Whether* we are born again and *how* we are born again stand as entirely different matters. It is possible for a person to think his is not born again because he has not had the dramatic experience, yet actually be born again. He may not understand the meaning of *born again*. It is an *education* issue, not a *spiritual* issue. It is equally true a person may have some sort of dramatic experience but not be born again. The reality and the perception may differ.

CULTURAL EXPECTATIONS

Our Christian culture places a premium on the dramatic conversion. We tend to equate new birth with the dramatic conversion, even though they are different. The plain fact is that the dramatic conversion is a cultural expectation while being born again is a spiritual surrender to the kingdom of God.

When someone lacks the dramatic conversion, and he has mistakenly thought that dramatic conversion was the condition precedent to being born again, he naturally objects. But this objection is more a cultural protest than a spiritual one. It is a reaction to the emphasis on dramatic conversion.

OSMOSIS IN THE CHRISTIAN HOME

Many Christians were raised in the kind of Christian home in which they can never remember not being a Christian. Theirs has been an almost imperceptible conversion that comes by being immersed in a Christian environment. It's the kind of conversion that slowly absorbs into the heart, soul, and mind, rather than one giant, dramatic leap out of a pagan lifestyle.

Those who grow up Christian certainly must make their own independent profession of faith in Christ—but when they do, they will see no blinding light. They have already been walking in the light.

The pagan sees blinding light because he walks from total darkness into light. A pagan's conversion is like a flash bulb unexpectedly going off in his eyes. But the one who grew up Christian merely walks from the well-lit anteroom into an even brighter dining room, where he sups with the Savior personally.

Both the dramatic conversion and the conversion by osmosis have their unmistakable moment of surrender. But the believer converted by osmosis over a long period probably cannot identify that unmistakable moment. It doesn't matter. Both are born again.

Some think that unless there is drama there is no new birth. The issue is not drama, but personal faith. "'The Son of Man must be lifted up, that everyone who believes in him may have eternal life'" (John 3:14–15). Everyone who truly and earnestly repents of his sins and receives Christ the Savior by faith is born again.

Because my friend doesn't think he is born again doesn't mean he is not. Rather, it means two things. First, he has had no dramatic conversion to which he can point (the cultural expectation). And second, he is uneducated to the fact that a dramatic conversion is unnecessary.

Have you struggled with the term, *born again*? If you have received Christ, dramatically or not, you are born again. It is the condition precedent to "see the kingdom of God" (v.3).

Have you denied the authenticity of someone's faith because he cannot point to his unmistakable moment—to a dramatic conversion? Have you denied your own new birth because you have been taunted? The issue is not drama, but personal faith. Do not place a cultural expectation upon people which Jesus does not require.

I SURRENDER

Lord Jesus, I have been mistaken in my understanding of what it means to be born again. Thank you that I am born again. Help me to be more sensitive to the faith of others. Amen.

If you are not born again, and would like to be, express your desire to Christ something like this: *Lord Jesus, I have reached my own unmistakable moment. I thank You for dying for my sins. I confess my sins to You, and ask You to forgive me. Take control of my life, sup with me, make me into the kind of person You want me to be. Amen.*

EIGHTEEN

Eternal Life:
The Undone Thing

"Teacher, what good thing must I do to get eternal life?"
Matthew 19:16

The rich young man asked Jesus the right question. What good thing must he do to get eternal life? Jesus replied, "...'If you want to enter life, obey the commandments.' 'Which ones?' the man inquired" (Matthew 19:17–18). Jesus listed them off.

"'All these I have kept,'" the young man said. "'What do I still lack?'" (v.20).

He sensed it. He knew intuitively that even though he kept the commandments there was still something left undone, something which was keeping him from eternal life. Why else would he inquire further?

Jesus then told him if he wanted to be perfect—to be complete—to sell his possessions, give to the poor, and follow Him. Jesus knew the undone thing which separated the man from devotion to Himself. He knows the undone thing which separates everyone from devotion to Himself.

With Jesus, the terms of eternal life are a total surrender of our lives to Him. Jesus always holds to one central idea in salvation: "'Follow me'" (v.21). But He knows the hidden ambition in each of us, the area which has become our stumbling stone. For the rich man, it may be his riches; for the poor man, his poverty.

Jesus doesn't offer eternal life in exchange for selling your possessions. Jesus offers eternal life in exchange for following Himself. The rich young man was not following Jesus. Jesus knew why—his possessions stood in the way. His attitude toward possessions formed an invisible barrier which blocked him from following Christ. His curse was not the visible barrier of his possession, but the invisible barrier of his attitude toward them. It represented the undone thing between him and a full surrender to Jesus. Is there an undone thing blocking you?

SELLING EVERYTHING GETS YOU NOWHERE

In this story we always focus on selling the possessions as the positive thing done. Here's the key point: Selling the possessions is not the positive thing done. Instead, for this man, selling them was only the removal of the negative thing which blocked a full surrender to Jesus.

The surrender to Christ is the positive thing done. For the rich young man, selling his possessions was his undone thing. Christ wasn't focused on what a good thing it would be for him to sell his possessions, but on what thing was left undone. Have you left anything undone? Do the undone thing. "'Then come, follow me'" (v.21).

We think we must do a good work before we can follow Jesus. Not so. The selling of possessions did not represent adding a good work that led to salvation, but removing an obstacle which blocked faith. "'What good thing must I do to get eternal life?'"—"'follow me.'"

Jesus placed no stock in the selling of possessions. Its only value was that it would remove the obstacle which kept the young man from the faith to follow Him. If a thing keeps you from the "follow me," then get rid of it. But Jesus never asked for a good work to get eternal life.

Faith saves, not works. The sale of his possessions alone would not have been enough to save him. Jesus said, "Then come, follow me." It is the "follow me," that saves. If a person can do the "follow me," without the need to sell his possessions, then Christ does not require it of the person. But there will be some other undone thing which needs doing.

Whatever the thing is that blocks us from following Him is the very thing that Jesus asks us to shed ourselves of, not as the adding of a positive but as the removal of a negative. To follow Jesus leads to eternal life. To sell possessions has no merit in itself, but it does have value if it removes the obstacle which keeps us from following Him.

The rich young man went away sad. He was no casual inquirer—this man had kept all the commandments. He was a sincere seeker. Eternal life was his goal. He asked the right question, but struggled with the answer.

I suspect this rich young man already knew the undone thing in his life. I suspect that before he asked Christ he knew his affections for his money made him stumble. Why else would he have kept pursuing Jesus with questions? When Jesus told him to keep the commandments, why was he not overjoyed? Why did he ask if there was more? He asked because in his heart of hearts he knew he had left a thing undone.

Have you left a thing undone? The essential question surfaces by itself: What do I still lack? What impediment to true faith is blocking you? For some, it is money. But for others it may be lifestyle, morals, temper, substance abuse, a secret thought life of lust and fantasy, personal ambitions, impure thoughts, selfishness, or wrong motives. Don't let it block you; lay it at the foot of the cross.

What is that thing which separates you from perfect devotion to Christ? Your relationship with Him would be perfect, were it not for this one thing. Do you want to believe, but giving up that thing brings sad thoughts to your mind? Give it up. Surrender it to Jesus. Do not stumble over such a small thing. Do not leave the undone thing undone. "Then come, follow me."

I SURRENDER

Jesus, I know that undone thing that has blocked me from following You. I surrender it to You now, by faith, to do with as You please. I offer it not as a good work which leads to salvation, but as the removal of the negative which has blocked me from following You. Thank You for dying on the cross for my sins. I acknowledge that I am a sinner and confess my sins. By faith, I receive You as my Savior and Lord. Take control of my life, and make me into the kind of person You want me to be. Thank You that by this action—faith and faith alone—You grant me eternal life, purpose and meaning. Amen.

NINETEEN

Assurance: Assurance of Salvation

The Spirit himself testifies with our spirit that we are God's children.

Romans 8:16

One of Florida's senior statesmen, a distinguished gentle-man in his sixties, exhorted me to spend time with my father. "When he is gone you will really miss him," he said.

His father had recently died, and I could literally feel his heartache as he mourned the loss of his natural father.

"Fathers are imperfect," he continued, "but they are so important to us. My dad, for example, was not much for showing affection. He never once gave me his approval when I was growing up. This caused me to always be striving to measure up—to get a nod from my dad. It didn't come. So I redoubled my efforts and worked to get better grades. Nothing. Then I worked on my career and became extremely successful. Still no approval.

"It was not until I was elected as an elder in my church that my father ever gave me his approval. He had been an elder in the same church for decades. As I knelt to be accepted, my father reached over, finally, after all those years, put his hand on my shoulder and said, 'I'm proud of you, son.' I burst into tears. That was one of the sweetest moments of my entire life. Fathers are not perfect, but when he is gone you will really miss him."

Did your father ever give you his approval? Or do you still long for your dad to say, "I'm proud of you, son."

THE NEED FOR APPROVAL

The need for approval is the unintended, hidden motivator behind so much of what we do. Whether from our father, our mother, our spouse, our children, our peers, our friends, or our boss: the need for approval is a silent, inescapable influence upon our lives. The nod from dad, the embrace from mother, respect from our spouse, appreciation from the boss for a job well done. Most of us, if we will be honest, are starving for human dignity. Nothing reduces us to loneliness and indignity faster than withheld approval.

Our Eternal Father and God loves us with an unconditional, everlasting love. And He does not love us because we have done anything to win His approval, anything to deserve it. Rather, He loves you because He made you. Have you grasped the magnitude of that love yet?

When once we have placed our faith and trust in Christ and His atoning work for us on the cross, then nothing can separate us from the approval of the Father. "My sheep listen to my voice; I know them, and they follow me. I give them eternal life, and they shall never perish; no one can snatch them out of my hand" (John 10:27–28). The approval of God secures salvation. Your earthly father may never say, "I'm proud of you," but your heavenly Father will personally wipe away every tear of yours someday. You have His Word on it. Approved, and secure forever.

Have you accepted the approval of the Father? Do you have the assurance of your salvation? Do you have confidence that your faith has saved you? Or does the drone of doubt still whisper its menacing monologue to your mind?

ETERNAL APPROVAL

If you have sincerely repented of your sins and received Jesus Christ by faith as your Savior and Lord, then you are immortal and eternal now, by the grace of the living Lord. You have His approval. Jesus said, "And this is the will of him who sent me, that I shall lose none of all that he has given me, but raise them up at the last day. For my Father's will is that everyone who looks to the Son and believes in him shall have eternal life" (John 6:39–40).

We are saved by faith, not works. His approval of us isn't contingent upon doing something to be good enough. He loves us because He made us. If your loved ones, only creatures, have withheld their approval, know that God works differently. If your loved ones continue to make you feel guilt, know that Christ's blood was shed for the removal of guilt. Once you have received Him, your sins are washed away—not by any merit on your part, but solely on the basis of your faith.

What, then, is the motivation to do good works? It is not to gain the approval of the Father. Those in Christ already have His approval. Rather, we are motivated to do good works out of the gratitude of a thankful heart. Because He justified us, we love to obey and please Him. We don't obey Him to please Him so we can receive justification. Justification (salvation) is by faith alone. Then, with heartfelt gratitude, the surrendered saint joyfully serves Christ.

KNOWING ASSURANCE PERSONALLY

Have you heard the voice of the Spirit? "The Spirit himself testifies with our spirit that we are God's children" (Romans 8:16). The authority of Scripture is the basis of our assurance. If you have received Christ, shut your eyes. Say to yourself, "I belong to Jesus. I am a child of God."

Do you sense harmony with that thought? That is the Spirit testifying with your spirit that you are a child of God. He loves you with an everlasting love. You belong to Him. He approves of you. He made you. The sense of assurance swelling within you is the Spirit Himself testifying with your own spirit that you are born again. You are welcome in the sanctum sanctorum. Abandon your plans to win His approval. At the instant you first surrendered, He approved you unconditionally.

I SURRENDER

My Father and my God, I confess that I have struggled to gain Your affection and approval. I know that I can never do anything to be good enough to win Your love. Instead, You love me because You made me. I surrender my doubts and my guilt to You, and I pray that You will remove them from my life. Thank you, Jesus, for dying on the cross for my sins, and for giving me eternal life. Because of You alone, I know that I have eternal life, that I will not be lost, that I will never perish. I know because of the authority of Your Word and the Spirit who testifies with my spirit. Amen.

PART FOUR

The World of My Motives

Nothing is easier than self-deceit. For what each man wishes, that he also believes to be true.

Demosthenes

TWENTY

Ambition: Fifteen Minutes at the Top

Send forth your light and your truth, let them guide me; let them bring me to your holy mountain, to the place where you dwell.

Psalm 43:3

Mount Everest towers five and one-half miles above the face of the earth. The mystical mountain has lured countless adventurers to conjure up grandiose plans to scale its pallid peak.

George Mallory was once asked why he wanted to ascend Everest's summit. "Because it is there!" came his revealing response. The ambition to conquer, to achieve, to excel—it has driven men.

Edmund Hillary and Tenzing Norgay, his guide, led the first successful assault against the intrepid Everest. Week after week they inched up the face of the world's tallest temptation. Herculean odds opposed them. Avalanches threatened to claim their very lives. Deep crevasses resisted negotiation. High winds howled their haunting warnings. Extreme steepness defied their ingenuities. Thin air sapped their strength.

As they ascended they continued to build new camps. Each of the seven succeeding camps grew smaller as more and more of the expedition team retreated from the severe strain of the immobile, inflexible pinnacle.

In his autobiography, Edmund Hillary described the exhilaration of becoming the first to arrive at Everest's apex. At 11:45 A. M. on May 29, 1953 Hillary and Norgay stood on top of the world.

But here's the interesting point. Fifteen minutes after they arrived, the raw fury of naked nature forced them to begin their descent. As Hillary recorded in his diary, unless they began the retreat back down the precipice to their base camp immediately, nightfall would overtake them and they would perish in the elements. Fifteen minutes at the top. All of that effort and sacrifice to stand for fifteen minutes on top of the world.

Almost everyone has their Everest, some goal to scale the upper heights, some ambition to make it to the top, some motive to walk among the great. People often describe their search for human dignity along the line of climbing the peak of a temporal summit. Human dignity actually is found on a mountain, but it is the holy mountain of God.

Most men climb the wrong mountain. As the cliché says, "I climbed my ladder to the top, only to find out it was leaning against the wrong wall." Is it worth it? Is fifteen minutes on top of the temporal world worth the price paid?

When men pursue selfish ambitions, they invariably climb a corporeal mountain where no man may rest. It is a mountain of loneliness. When Christ ascended into the mountains His goal was never His self-will. Rather, He went there to meet with the Father. The only mountain worth climbing is the one which ascends to the Father.

The goal of the Christian life is to ascend the holy hill. It is to surrender the self-will of ambition which strives for human achievement at the expense of knowing God personally. The independent spirit wants Everest. The surrendered spirit wants the holy hill. The essential question is, "Who may ascend the hill of the Lord? Who may stand in his holy place?" (Psalm 24:3). Jesus offers a passport to the holy hill, to a mountain of rest.

Everyone has his Everest. Do you have some mountain of ambition you are trying to scale? Only a weary few stand at the top. And even those, after fifteen minutes of glory, are forced by the laws of nature to descend. The older men must make way for the younger ones—they, too want their fifteen minutes at the top. Is it worth it?

Are you climbing the wrong mountain? Are you ascending a hill where you can dwell with God, or will your mountain offer fifteen minutes of fame? If you have been climbing the wrong mountain, ask God to redirect your ambition. He will refocus your affections on Himself.

If you have been climbing a temporal mountain—a mountain of selfish ambition, God wants you to retreat. Locate His holy hill on the map of your mind. Find Him, for He lives on a mountain great and high. "Exalt the Lord our God and worship at his holy mountain, for the Lord our God is holy" (Psalm 99:9). It is a mountain from which we need never descend. The choice is fifteen minutes or forever.

I Surrender

Holy Father, I have been climbing a mountain of selfish ambition. I have been climbing the wrong mountain, looking for fifteen minutes at the top. I surrender my selfish ambitions to You and ask You to forgive me for my folly. Send forth Your light and Your truth, let them guide me; let them bring me to Your holy mountain, to the place where You dwell. Show me how I may ascend Your holy hill and worship You acceptably. Amen.

TWENTY-ONE

Approval: Man-Pleasers and God-Pleasers

Am I now trying to win the approval of men, or of God? Or am I trying to please men?

Galatians 1:10

I asked myself, *Why am I always so edgy about my accomplishments when I am around Steve? Why am I always trying to prove myself to him? What is it that I am trying to prove, anyway?*

We all have friends like that, people around whom we feel a need to perform if we are to gain their approval and friendship. When we're with them, we feel tempted to rehearse all of our accomplishments. Why? Because intuitively we know that is how they rate us.

And we all have had a friend who always tells us every thing he has ever done. Why is that? What motivates these kinds of behavior?

The need for approval—to be accepted and appreciated—silently forms a backdrop behind every scene played out upon the stage of life. The need for approval is inseparably fused into every decision we make, every response we give, every task we perform, every interpretation we make of what people do and say to us. So what is wrong with that? Is it such a sin to want to be liked?

Every form of aberrant behavior reveals a trace of the need for approval gone unmet. Whether marital infidelity, substance abuse, child or spouse abuse, depression, suicide, anger on the roadways, paralyzing fears, or withdrawal from friends—some need for approval gone unmet will be found. The unmet need for approval makes us sensitive to the perceived slight from a friend. It drives us to accomplish great feats so that we will gain needed appreciation from our peers.

PLEASING MEN

If our self-worth rests solely upon the approval of men, we will soon wither to dust and blow away. The approval of men is not dependable. Men will take but not return. If the focus of your labor is to please and be approved by men, you will alternate between the fatigue of trying to please unpleasable masters and the disillusionment of completing thankless tasks. Still, the need for approval—to be accepted and appreciated—is compelling.

Our need for approval is the need for human dignity. The problem is that people don't accept and appreciate us as we are, simply because of our humanity. They want more.

People approve of us only when our performance meets their expectations. A minimum threshold must be reached before they will approve us. We please men by crossing over the threshold; then they will offer their approval. But if once your performance slips below the minimum line, we are out again. That's a tough way to live, a high pressure lifestyle, and a formula for disillusionment and a poor self-image. When performance is the standard of approval, human dignity is reduced to the level of a performing seal.

To gain the needed approval and dignity, most of us conform. We learn how the system works and give people what they want: performance. But just as the motive of people is sin, so is our response. It is the way of the world, and not the way of God.

PLEASING GOD

God calls us to gain His approval, not man's. "Am I now trying to win the approval of men, or of God?" (Galatians 1:10). God calls us to please Him, not men. "We are not trying to please men but God, who tests our hearts" (1 Thessalonians 2:4). Be a God-pleaser and not a man-pleaser.

How do we please God? How do we gain His approval? God's approval is conditioned only upon our faith and not upon our performance. That is how we please Him. Surely, out of a heart filled with gratitude we will want to do something to please God. But this is because we have already received His unconditional approval and acceptance. It is the grateful heart, not the pressure to perform for approval, that motivates the Christian to please God.

When you and I focus upon pleasing God, our motives for performing change. Instead of contending for prestige and honor, we surrender our very being to the God who created us. Our desire is for His desire.

We become soaked in the knowledge of His will and purpose. We rest in Him because He says simply, "Come to me." His approval is unconditioned. That was settled upon the cross, and our faith in it. Gratitude motivates our performance, not approval. Dignity, approval, and appreciation motivate men to please men through performance, but Christ gives them freely for the asking.

How have you been a man-pleaser instead of a God-pleaser? Have you conditioned your self-worth upon the approval of men—men who will withhold that approval until you have measured up to their expectations? Redirect your efforts to please God.

I Surrender

Lord, I confess that I have been more motivated by the approval of men than by my desire to please You. As a result, my self-worth is low, because I have not measured up to the expectations of sinful men. Thank you that You have already given me Your approval. Revive me, Lord, and grant me a spirit of gratitude for the dignity You give freely to me by faith in Your finished work on the cross. Amen.

TWENTY-TWO

Devotion: Fully Devoted to God

As Solomon grew old ... his heart was not fully devoted to the Lord his God.

1 Kings 11:4

Is your heart "fully" devoted to the Lord? The Lord loved Solomon deeply. Solomon's ways pleased the Lord; so much so that the Lord offered, "Ask for whatever you want me to give you" (1 Kings 3:5).

At Solomon's request, the Lord gave him wisdom and knowledge, but added to it wealth, riches, and honor "such as no king who was before you ever had and none after you will have" (2 Chronicles 1:12).

And what was the condition placed upon Solomon to enjoy this undeserved blessing? "And if you walk in my ways and obey my statutes and commands as David your father did, I will give you a long life" (1 Kings 3:14).

The way of Solomon prospered. He finished building the temple of the Lord. "God gave Solomon wisdom and very great insight, and a breadth of understanding as measureless as the sand on the seashore. . . . He was wiser than any other man" (1 Kings 4:29,31).

Of his stature the Queen of Sheba said, "The report I heard in my own country about your achievements and your wisdom is true. But I did not believe these things until I came and saw with my own eyes. Indeed, not even half was told me; in wisdom and wealth you have far exceeded the report I heard" (1 Kings 10:6–7). "King Solomon was greater in riches and wisdom than all the other kings of the earth" (1 Kings 10:23).

God loved Solomon; however.... The word "however" ranks among the most pregnant of words. It qualifies whatever has gone before it. It is a modifier. It changes the good report to a conditional report, or softens the blow of a bad report.

"King Solomon, *however*, loved many foreign women" (1 Kings 11:1, emphasis added). In this instance, the word *however* recasts the greatest report ever given into a sad light. About other nations the Lord instructed, "'You must not intermarry with them, because they will surely turn your hearts after their gods.' Nevertheless, Solomon held fast to them in love" (1 Kings 11:2).

Solomon remained true to only God for many years, but because he intermarried with the culture of the world, he later turned to other gods and "his heart was not *fully* devoted to the Lord his God ..." (1 Kings 11:4, emphasis added).

"Fully" is another one of those pregnant words inflated with implications. Yes, he still served God, but he merged other beliefs into his way. How was he not "fully" devoted? He also followed Ashtoreth and Molech.

Ashtoreth was the goddess of sensual living, sexual license, and free love. Molech was the detestable god to whom child sacrifices were made. Sound familiar? Our land, ripped and torn by less-than-full devotion to God, has turned its heart after these very same gods.

Sensual living. Abortion. If it feels good, do it. Is it any wonder that "the Lord became angry with Solomon because his heart had turned away" (1 Kings 11:9)? Is it any wonder that the Lord is angry with America, whose heart is not fully devoted to Him?

Solomon's life was going along fine until he came to his "however." To walk in God's ways and obey God's statutes was his delight, until he came to his "however." Solomon's "however" was his love of foreign women. He yielded to it, he intermarried with them, the very thing God asked him not to do. God warns against giving in to our "howevers." "You must not intermarry with them, because they will *surely* turn your hearts after their gods." It is a cause and effect relationship. Have you intermarried with the culture? Have you given in to the "however" of your life?

Solomon died a broken man, disillusioned and spiritually insensible. He thought he could have it both ways. He merged the way of God with the way of the world, and the world swallowed him up.

Is your heart fully devoted to the Lord your God? Or have you intermarried? Flee from the gods of this broken world. Flee, before they swallow you up. Are you wiser than Solomon? He could not serve both Ashtoreth and God, both Molech and the Lord. Plead with the one true God for grace to free your from the snare. Dare you risk it? Are you thinking to yourself, *I can get away with this because it's not hurting me right now?*

It is easier to continue with the Lord than it is to make a comeback. Be on guard. Do you want to grow old with dignity? Relearn His ways; make sure you have them right. "'If you walk in my ways and obey my statutes and commands.... I will give you a long life'" (1 Kings 3:14).

In our day millions of Christians have been swallowed up by the world. They have intermarried with the culture. They worship God but are not fully devoted to Him—they wink at the false gods of Solomon's day: the goddess of sensual living and the god of child sacrifices (abortion).

Sensual living, materialism, legalism, pop religion, abortion, drugs, liberalism, emotionalism, relative values: These are the "howevers"—the other gods—of this age. The result? Millions of us are ending up disillusioned and spiritually insensible—divorced, chemically dependent, bitter, and apostate.

The only solution is to surrender to the God who is. The turning point of our lives is when we stop seeking the God we want and start seeking the God who is. A total re-surrender is the antidote for the heart not fully devoted to God.

I Surrender

Dear Father, the one true God. My life is filled with "howevers." My heart has not been fully devoted to You. I confess that I have intermarried with the culture, and I am headed toward disillusionment and spiritual insensibility. Revive my spirit, O God. Forgive my stubborn way. Do not let me be swallowed up by the world. Forgive me and fill me with the Holy Spirit. Empower me to walk in Your ways and to obey Your statutes. Amen.

PART FIVE

The Art of Surrender

*There is a moment of surrender and a
process of surrender. The moment of
surrender is the surrender of the will
to personal belief in Jesus, that He is the crucified
Savior who forgives sin. It is the moment of faith.
It happens in an instant of time.*

*The process of surrender is the lifelong, daily
crucifying of the human will—the will of the
flesh—over and over and over again. It is
surrender and resurrender and re-resurrender. It is
a "process" because we surrender our will at the
foot of the cross, but then we take it back up again.
Surrender is an art.*

TWENTY-THREE

Surrender: The Process of Surrender

"If anyone would come after me, he must deny himself and take up his cross daily and follow me."

Luke 9:23

John's wife sarcastically called down from her loft studio, "I see you are watching another one of those Christian movies."

Actually, John was watching another sizzling sex-packed, profanity-permeated action movie on pay television, one whose seamy scenes would have made people blush twenty-five years ago.

His wife's comment jolted him like a lightning bolt. He had been a committed Christian for several years, but he still struggled with many areas of his life which he had presumed would self-correct after his initial surrender to Christ.

John realized his wife had unearthed another unguarded, unexamined area of his life which was unsurrendered. He could cancel his pay television, but he still wondered how he could be a Christian and continue to have so many blindspots.

Surrender is a daily task. "'If anyone would come after me, he must ... take up his cross *daily* and follow me'" (Luke 9:23, emphasis added). There is a moment of surrender and a process of surrender.

THE MOMENT VERSUS THE PROCESS

The moment of surrender is the surrender of the will to personal belief in Jesus, that He is the crucified Savior who forgives sin. It is the moment of faith. It happens in an instant of time.

The process of surrender is the lifelong, daily crucifying of the human will—the will of the flesh—over and over and over again. It is surrender and resurrender and *re*-resurrender. It is a process because we surrender our will at the foot of the Cross, but then we take it back up again.

The will of the flesh is an ugly ogre, a toady troll. He lurks in the shadows of every decision. His lackeys inject themselves like poisons into the stream of our conscious thoughts. Their names are pride, independence, envy, self-sufficiency, slander, individualism, jealousy, self-determination, autonomy, and self-reliance. Jesus said, "'For from within, out of men's hearts, come evil thoughts, sexual immorality, theft, murder, adultery, greed, malice, deceit, lewdness, envy, slander, arrogance and folly'" (Mark 7:21–22).

Because of the will of the flesh, we must participate in continual, daily surrender. It is to yield, to submit, to abandon to Christ, and to do so every day. It is to relinquish our right to have our own way, and to do so daily. It is on-going conversion to daily obedience.

Conversion does not take place in the blinking of an eye. Conversion occurs on a time line. Let's face it, if we knew everything about ourselves that God wanted to change, we would blow all our circuit breakers. We couldn't handle knowing how God sees us all at once. We are converted to salvation in a moment of time, but our conversion to obedience is a lifelong process of daily surrender. "Continue to work out your salvation with fear and trembling" (Philippians 2:12).

A THINKING SURRENDER

To surrender does not mean that we surrender our minds, but our wills. To surrender the will does not mean to resign the intellect. On the contrary, the sharpened mind aids the process of surrender. It is the thinking mind which examines itself. Only thinking people advance themselves, either toward self-interests or surrender. The active mind penetrates the depths for truth while the dull mind wallows in puddles of shallow thinking.

While some Christians are eager to be fully converted, the tendency is to linger with the old ways. The inertia of the existing lifestyle is the adversary of total surrender. Before believing in Christ, we spent all our energies to build a comfortable, prosperous life. It is painful to admit our own errors, so we let the old lifestyle linger.

Christ may or may not ask you to change your lifestyle, but He does command you to surrender it to Him, and to do so daily. "'He must deny himself and take up his cross daily and follow me.'" Where is Jesus going that He wants you to follow Him? Are you in His footsteps?

Do you want to follow Jesus? Do you want to live a life of full, total, complete surrender to Christ? Then you must deny the will of the flesh. Be filled with the Holy Spirit. Take up your cross daily, crucifying afresh the ugly ogre of your selfish desires. If anyone would come after Him, these things he must do. Every other path leads to *un*surrender.

Never hold out in an area that Jesus reveals is unsurrendered. To hold out scuffles with the process of surrender. We are converted to faith in a moment of surrender, but we are converted to obedience over a lifetime by surrendering afresh each day. First comes the moment of surrender, then the process of surrender. "'If anyone would come after me, he must deny himself and take up his cross daily and follow me'" (Luke 9:23).

I Surrender

Father, I confess that my lifestyle has created an inertia against proceeding toward a full surrender. I desire to advance with You, Lord, to complete the process of surrender. Today I deny myself, take up my cross, and follow You. Show me where You are going. Empower me with the Holy Spirit to surrender myself to You each and every day. I want to live a life characterized by obedient surrender. Amen.

TWENTY-FOUR

Impulsiveness: Good Ideas Versus God Ideas

Peter said to Jesus, "Lord, it is good for us to be here. If you wish, I will put up three shelters—one for you, one for Moses and one for Elijah."

Matthew 17:4

The natural inclination in Christian living is to act on the impulse of a good idea. Not every good idea is from God. Sometimes good ideas get in the way of God ideas.

Where does your inspiration come from? The vision of the transfigured Christ inspired Peter: "'Lord, it is good for us to be here. If you wish, I will put up three shelters—one for you, one for Moses and one for Elijah'" (Matthew 17:4). Our natural impulse is to do something good for Him. We make a plan to do something good for God and suggest it to Him.

The tendency of the well-meaning person is to prepare a plan to do some good idea, and then pray, "Jesus, this is my plan. It is a good plan. It hurts no one, and I want it to please you. Lord, please bless my plan." It is plan, then pray.

So many of our ideas are impetuous. They are not what the Lord wants to do. They do not resemble in any way the things which concern Him. We have good ideas, but they are not God ideas. His agenda and our agenda conflict. We want to build Him a shelter, but that is not what He wants. "While he was *still speaking*, a bright cloud enveloped them" (Matthew 17:5, emphasis added), and God spoke, ignoring Peter as though he were not even there. Peter's idea was so impetuous that God interrupted Peter—didn't even let him finish.

When Peter, James, and John heard the voice of the Lord, "they fell facedown to the ground, terrified" (Matthew 17:6). They abandoned their inventive-but-self-made idea. The presence of the Lord magnified, and His holiness brought them to their senses. Jesus gained their attention, not by subduing them with a stern scolding, but by magnifying His presence until all the genius of their human ideas was bleached out by His refulgent face. When they abandoned their good idea and fell facedown before the Lord, He could work with them again. "But Jesus came and touched them. 'Get up,' he said. 'Don't be afraid'" (Matthew 17:7).

When you and I abandon our good idea and fall to our face before the Lord, then He will come and touch us, too. When we pursue our own plan, He cannot use us. We must abandon our good idea and fall facedown before Him. Then He will be able to use us again. Then He will reveal what He is doing—a God idea. "As they came down the mountain, Jesus instructed them" (Matthew 17:9). It is pray, then plan. Through prayer, Jesus instructs of His plan, a God idea.

Prayer removes the impulse of the good idea, the good idea born of human ingenuity but not of God. Pray, then plan. It is the habit of the surrendered saint.

I SURRENDER

Lord, I must confess that my way has been "plan, then pray." I have wanted to do good things for You; my motives have been to please You. But I realize that I have built shelters You didn't need, and never used. I have wasted so much valuable time on matters that don't matter. I surrender all my plans to You, Lord. I will forget them. I will pray, then plan. I will pray and wait for You to come and touch me and say, "Get up. Don't be afraid." I am listening now, Lord. Instruct me with Your plan. Amen.

TWENTY-FIVE

Significance: About Being Busy

What does a man get for all the toil and anxious striving with which he labors under the sun?

Ecclesiastes 2:22

It was one of the busy times. The phone rang off the hook. Everybody wanted to talk to Chuck. On one hand, it was immensely frustrating, but at the same time, it made him feel vital and needed. Although his stress level shot up, the busyness gave him a feeling of importance.

The longing we each have to feel significant is a beguiling, hard-to-understand but very real need. When we are wanted or needed by others, we feel this need is being met. Often, however, we become busy but don't actually do anything very significant. We can become busy and feel good about ourselves, but our busyness may not contribute very much to forever.

VALUE VERSUS VELOCITY

The trap of busyness is that we tend to equate the value of our labor with the velocity of our labor—how busy we are. In truth, busyness does not lead to significance, but to self-importance.

Busy people become puffed up with themselves. They feel important because so many people want to speak with them. In reality, very few of these people care about you as a person. They will not cry at your funeral. They will not help you when your fortunes change. They will eat your food and drink your wine, but they will soon forget your name.

Labor which God our Father approves is born in your private watch before Christ. It is not puffed up in self-importance. It does not seek to be busy to feel important, it seeks to be busy for the glory of God.

The only significant work is preassigned by the Father. "For we are God's workmanship, created in Christ Jesus to do good works, which God has prepared *in advance* for us to do" (Ephesians 2:10, emphasis added). We must kneel at the cross and patiently wait for God to reveal His important work. This kind of watch leads a man to a measured sort of labor—a considered, controlled form of busyness that leads to a destiny of true significance.

IMPATIENCE

Most people do not wait. They rush headlong into worthwhile but self-made works. Most people, impatient to find true significance, become busy. In practice, they become self-important. Busyness is a curse of the devil. So what does the busy person receive for all their toil and striving? "All his days his work is pain and grief; even at night his mind does not rest" (Ecclesiastes 2:23).

When you start to get busy: Stop. Ask yourself: "Does this busyness flow from the work God has revealed to me? Or am I merely busy, searching impatiently for strokes to make me feel good about myself?" The one who searches for strokes has received his reward in full.

THE REWARD OF PATIENCE

The person who slows down to hear the whisper of the Holy Spirit will labor in significance. The world may not recognize the importance of his good works, but the Spirit will testify with his spirit that it is the work God prepared in advance for him to do. "To the man who pleases him, God gives wisdom, knowledge and happiness" (Ecclesiastes 2:26).

I SURRENDER

My Father, I confess that I have often been more interested in feeling good about myself than in knowing Your will. I have been consumed in busyness, and I have not been still before You. I have created a world of self-importance, but I am not doing enough that is truly significant—things that will last forever. I surrender my busyness to You, Lord. Reveal to me that good work which You prepared in advance for me to do. And I will wait patiently for it—for months, even years, if that is Your desire. Amen.

TWENTY-SIX

Trustability: Remember What Is in You

But Jesus would not entrust himself to them, for he knew all men. He did not need man's testimony about man, for he knew what was in a man.

John 2:24–25

In his heart he had often pondered the question he was about to ask. God's material blessing upon his life was abundant, and he didn't know why. He openly wondered to a close friend, "I don't understand why God has blessed me this way?" The friend's immediate and unhesitating response came, "Because He knows He can trust you."

He treasured those words, much as he imagined Mary treasured the words of the angel Gabriel. He knew he had integrity, that God could trust him when he was alone. The mistake, though, was to assume that because he could be trusted that his human nature was therefore trustworthy.

Yes, at our core we can have the desire for a pure heart, to be godly, to have integrity, to be trustworthy but, as Paul says, "So I find this law at work: When I want to do good, evil is right there with me. For in my inner being I delight in God's law; but I see another law at work in the members of my body, waging war against the law of my mind" (Romans 7:21–23).

Our mistake is to believe that because we can be trusted at all that we are then absolutely trustworthy, as a matter of our nature in Christ. We don't know ourselves as Christ does. We lose the sense of our own capacity to be untrustable. We don't understand that in trust, as in all areas, the flesh wars against the Spirit. Our decisions became invincible in our own minds. The result: We stumble. We make poor choices because we think God's blessing is irrevocable, that our trustworthiness gives us tenure.

When God faithfully inflicts us, we will humble ourselves before Him, and trustworthiness will return. But this new sense of being trustable is mixed together with the absolute understanding that Christ never *fully* entrusts Himself to any man, because we each always have the capacity to sin at any moment. Yes, He can trust you, as long as you acknowledge that you understand you cannot be fully trusted, as long as you leave a sentinel posted on lookout for self-deceit. Remember what is in you.

I SURRENDER

Dear Father, how I long to be accepted by You, to be acceptable. I have strived to be trustworthy and loyal to You. But I have also become too sure of myself. I surrender my self-confidence to You and pray You will never again allow me to become smug and complacent toward the trust which You have placed in me. Amen.

TWENTY-SEVEN

Servanthood: In Search of Excellence

"He must become greater; I must become less."

John 3:30

I want to become an excellent speaker for God," I said to a close friend, after teaching a Bible study for two years. "I know that I am doing a good job, but I want to rise to the next level. Tell me, what do you think I need to work on to become excellent?"

"I think you are doing a great job," my friend replied. "Your gestures, your voice modulation, your syntax and structure, your eye contact—they're really . . ."

"You don't understand," I interrupted. "I can get anyone to say those things to me. But we're friends. What I need is for someone to take the risk and be totally honest with me. What do you really think I need to pass the threshold from good to excellent?"

"Well, I am telling you the truth. I think you are doing a great job. I couldn't recommend a single piece of advice for you to improve. But the move from good to excellent, only the Holy Spirit can do that."

The bulb flashed; the lights blinked on—instant truth. That was the elusive answer. The common sense way to make a bigger contribution focuses on strengthening skills. The Christ way focuses on the enabling Holy Spirit. Only the anointing of the Holy Spirit will move you to spiritual excellence.

The way to improve your contribution is to become more excellent. But spiritual greatness is not spiritual stardom; it is servanthood. God is looking for servants, not stars. The road to an improved contribution isn't moving up in the organization; it is surrendering your motives to the Holy Spirit. Is your desire to improve your contribution for personal prestige, or to garner glory for God?

Spiritual excellence is not about ascending the ladder of leadership to greatness. It is about descending the ladder of humility to servanthood. Let's face it. It is a difficult thing to be a leader and a servant at the same time, impossible without the Spirit. Lead and serve simultaneously? How? If a leader becomes a servile sycophant, then who would follow him?

The leader/servant is a man like John the Baptist. Though strong in personality and character, he understood his role. "He must become greater; I must become less."

Since learning that only the Holy Spirit can make one excellent, I have also discovered another secret. It is not that the Holy Spirit empowers a person to become more dynamic, eloquent, and persuasive—though all these may possibly come. Rather, it is that the Holy Spirit helps you to become nothing to yourself, you "become less." Not servile, but a servant.

Don't ask the Holy Spirit to increase your skill, ask Him to increase Christ. As Jesus becomes greater your impact will enlarge, but because Christ is growing larger, not you. John the Baptist did not shrink; Christ grew larger. He became less by letting Christ become more.

His goal for you is servanthood, not stardom. The servant no longer wants to become a great man of God; he wants to become less. His love for the Lord Jesus becomes such an intense fire that he abandons all desire to be liked, to do a good job, to have a winning way, to be a great man of God. He loses interest in who holds first place. He stakes out his claim on last place. His highest aim becomes for Christ to increase, for himself to decrease.

It had been a long day when Martin Luther King, Jr. stepped to the podium. All day long men had jockeyed for position on the speaking platform. The lawn of the Washington Mall teemed with thousands of potential ardent followers. One by one King deferred to the ambitious aspirants. One by one the crowd began to dwindle. It was the tail end of the day; things were tapering off.

When all others had their say, King took his slot at the end of the schedule. Holy passion coursed through his veins. With trembling voice he declared, "I have a dream."

Martin Luther King, Jr., went on to deliver the famous sermon which further entrenched him into the national conscience. Was it because he spoke last from the podium to a dwindling crowd? No, but because his ambition was to be a servant, never for himself. He understood that "He must become greater; I must become less." God can use people like that.

This is the highest plateau upon which the servant can serve. It is the old gospel—Christ high and lifted up, the bondslave to Christ never competing for center stage.

It is having the same attitude of Christ, taking on the very nature of a servant.

I SURRENDER

Father, I confess I have wanted to be a great man of God. I surrender my desire to be great, O God, and ask You to forgive me of my selfish ambition. Let me be filled with the power of Your Holy Spirit, and let me decrease. I will pursue excellence, not greatness; I will no longer confuse them to be the same but recognize them as opposites. Amen.

TWENTY-EIGHT

Expectations: Surrendering to Scripture

Delight yourself in the Lord and he will give you the desires of your heart.

Psalm 37:4

I have studied this passage regularly for about ten years. It is the only passage I can recall which has ever caused me to doubt the infallibility of the Word.

Early in my spiritual pilgrimage a saintly teacher pointed out the promise of Psalm 37:4. Immediately I began to appropriate this truth in my life for "the desires of my heart." I claimed this verse as a promise for a business deal here and a possession there. I delighted in the Lord, and waited patiently for Him to shower me with my heart's desires. Most of the time they never came.

Doubts about the authority and reliability of the Word crept in. So I checked the Bible out. What I learned overwhelmed me. The Bible comprises a collection of sixty-six separate books written on three continents, in three languages, over a fifteen hundred year time span by thirty-seven different human authors inspired by the Holy Spirit. These included kings and peasants, philosophers and fishermen, poets and statesmen, shepherds and soldiers. Even with such remarkable diversity, the Scriptures by far possess the greatest unity and continuity among the great works of literature.

Manuscript evidence harpoons criticism on that front. Whereas only five complete manuscripts of Aristotle and twelve of Plato exist—universally regarded as the two greatest philosophers of history—thirteen thousand New Testament manuscripts have survived the centuries.

There is not room to mention in detail archaeological evidence such as the Dead Sea Scrolls and the uncovering of forgotten kingdoms whose only record is the Bible. Nor does space allow to mention in detail three hundred fulfilled prophesies made four hundred to fifteen thousand years before Christ's first coming, nor the track record of the Bible's benefits to men and societies, nor the testimony of its authors.

After my investigation I chose to believe the Bible on faith. Not that I understood everything in it, but I accepted it was virtually impossible for such an incredible book to ever come into existence except by the hand of the Almighty. Still, Psalm 37:4 stalked me.

One morning a few years ago light exploded from this verse like brilliant flares from an electrical storm. I discovered that it was not that the verse was untrue, but that I had not yet penetrated the passage deeply enough.

I had not learned what the verse really meant. I had only superimposed my own expectations upon it. When it didn't deliver, I assumed the verse was in error, not me. While that may be conspicuously foolish now—even arrogant—at the time no other reaction even occurred to me.

The word *delight* comes from a Hebrew word that means "to be soft or pliable." So then, when we are to "delight" in the Lord we are to be soft or pliable. In other words, to delight in the Lord is to be clay in the potter's hands, to come humbly without heavy demands, to come eager to know the God who is and not the God we want, to come anxious for God to "make me" rather than for Him to "give me."

When I finally surrendered my expectations of Psalm 37:4 a chain reaction initiated. I started coming to the Lord with a new attitude, one of softness and pliability. Instead of telling God what my desires were, I came to understand Him. What is His character? What are His attributes? How can I worship Him more acceptably?

Then the amazing began. God began to grant my desires. But here is the trick: As I surrendered my expectations and "delighted" in Him, the desires of my heart began to change. Through my newfound pliability, He changed my desires by making His desires come alive in me. Over time, *His* desires actually became *my* desires. And when my desires were one with His desires in a given area, He would grant them. He granted them because they were actually His desires (His will) now alive in me as the delight of my own heart and mind.

There are no contradictions in Scripture. What is not understood is a paradox or a mystery, but not contradiction. The Word will always resolve its own apparent contradictions and enigmas, either in this life or the life to come. What we do not yet understand does not make the Bible invalid. It only means that God has not yet chosen to reveal a particular truth to us. We will know it all in due time.

Our expectations need to be altered, not our belief in Scripture's inerrancy. The Bible is not in error, we are.

Believe the Word, not men. "Stop trusting in man, who
has but a breath in his nostrils. Of what account is he?"
(Isaiah 2:22). We are vapors that appear for a little while
and then vanish, but the Word of God stands forever.

Are your expectations twisting the meaning of
Scripture? Do you come to God soft and pliable, seeking Him as He really is? Or have you not yet surrendered
your expectations to Him? Surrender your expectations
and delight in Him; then He will give you the desires of
your heart.

I SURRENDER

Dear God, I realize that I have superimposed selfish expectations onto the Bible and my personal
relationship with You. I know that You are who
You are, and that I must seek You as the God who
is, not as the God I want. I surrender my expectations to You and ask You to change the desires
of my heart until they are one with Yours. Amen.

TWENTY-NINE

The Holy Spirit: How to Strengthen a Willing Spirit

They did not know what to say to him.

Mark 14:40

When I am a good friend, I am a very good friend. But there are times when my friends would be better off without me.

One friend was sick for two weeks and I didn't even call him on the phone. Another friend went through a divorce, and I wasn't there for him. Still another friend received a great honor, but I never congratulated him. A friend stopped by to see me but I was tied up in a meeting, and I never tried to contact him later.

Sometimes we are the weakest of friends. We disappoint. Then, when we see that friend again we are embarrassed. We were not there for them when they needed us. We let them down. We do not know what to say.

When we are not a good friend, it is possible that we are being a selfish, wicked-hearted person. But the far more likely answer is that we are weak, not filled with the power of the Holy Spirit.

The disciples went out to Gethsemane to keep watch with Jesus while sorrow overwhelmed His soul. But they fell asleep. At the very moment their Friend needed them most, they were not there for Him. But these were not evil men; rather, they were weak. "'The spirit is willing, but the body is weak'" (Mark 14:38).

A second time Jesus went a short distance to pray. When He returned they had fallen asleep again, "because their eyes were heavy. They did not know what to say to him" (Mark 14:40). What could they say? They had let their Friend down, disappointed Him. Who among us has not let our Friend down in far greater ways?

Yet these men loved Jesus, just as you and I love Jesus. Their failure to stay awake with Jesus was not a despicable lack of compassion for their Friend. No, they, too, were "exhausted from sorrow" (Luke 22:45). Their bodies were weak from the grind of life. The stress of the moment had taken its toll. The physical and mental exhaustion from overwork had come upon them. And they fell asleep.

"They did not know what to say to him." The disciples did not know what to say to Jesus because they were embarrassed. They had fallen asleep not once but three times. Three opportunities to demonstrate their devotion to the Lord, three times failed. The Holy Spirit had not come upon them yet, and they did not know why they were weak. "The spirit is willing, but the body is weak." And so they did not know how to explain themselves.

Jesus did not accuse them of sin. But He did express disappointment that his friends were not there for Him, that they slept. "'Could you not keep watch for one hour?'" (Mark 14:37). How have you disappointed Christ? "Could you not keep watch for one hour?" We all let Him down. No matter, He knows the body is weak. But is your spirit willing? If it is not, ask Him to grant you a willing spirit that He might sustain you. You and I can strengthen our willing spirits. "But you will receive power when the Holy Spirit comes on you; and you will be my witnesses in Jerusalem, and in all Judea and Samaria, and to the ends of the earth" (Acts 1:8). Has the Holy Spirit come upon you? By this, I don't mean the indwelling of the Holy Spirit. Surely, all believers are indwelt with the Holy Spirit. But has the *power* of the Holy Spirit come upon you? Or, do you still fall asleep on your Friend? Is it time to grow up in your salvation to the point of walking in the power of the Holy Spirit every moment? Confess your sins, then, and ask Him to fill your willing spirit with the power of His Holy Spirit. "Fan into flame the gift of God" (2 Timothy 1:6).

Now walk in the Spirit, keeping watch, not letting your Friend down. And if you should fall asleep a second or third time, wake up, and start again. Soon you will walk in His Spirit's power more than you did at first.

I SURRENDER

Lord Jesus, I want to be a better friend. I confess that I have let You down, and after You have been my Friend. I do not know what to say to You. My spirit is willing, but my body is weak. Therefore, Lord, I ask you to fill me with the power of your Holy Spirit so that I might keep watch. Help me fan into flame the gift of Your Spirit. And when I fall asleep the second or third time, come to me and wake me, and I will try again. Amen.

PART SIX

The Tools of Surrender

God has equipped us with the means to submit to Christ in all the details of life.

THIRTY

Prayer: The Disposition to Pray

And pray in the Spirit on all occasions with all kinds of prayers and requests. With this in mind, be alert and always keep on praying for all the saints.

Ephesians 6:18

Is prayer your natural disposition? Is it your first line of thinking, behaving, and reacting? Or is prayer often only an afterthought?

Prayer is the currency of our personal relationship with Christ. It is the medium of exchange between needy people and a rich God. The man who is poor in relationships, destitute in hope, and hungry for significance can purchase them with prayer.

The possibilities of prayer form the hidden asset not listed on the balance sheet of every one of us. Prayer made in faith is the currency we can offer for the need we have. The man or woman who is rich in prayer is very rich. "The prayer of a righteous man is powerful and effective" (James 5:16). Without prayer, though, the soul languishes in poverty. What is the best reason to pray?

THE SILHOUETTE OF JESUS

The first disposition of Jesus was to pray. Prayer was how He collected Himself, how He gathered His mind. "But Jesus often withdrew to lonely places and prayed" (Luke 5:16).

Draw in your mind a silhouette of our cherished Lord. Is He not talking to the Father?—it was His first disposition. The goal of Christian life is to be like Jesus. The best reason to pray is that Jesus prayed. When we pencil ourselves inside His silhouette, when we retrace our temperament to fit within the outline of His disposition, we will pray.

How did Jesus pray? Jesus did not pray about everything. He prayed for people. He did not pray for material wealth, nicer vacations, better clothes, and a job promotion. He prayed for His disciples, for those who would believe through their message (us), for the needs of people, and for the will of His Father.

Jesus loved to pray—it was the natural disposition of His temperament:

> Very early in the morning, while it was still dark, Jesus got up, left the house and went off to a solitary place, where he prayed. (Mark 1:35)

> He went up on a mountainside by himself to pray. When evening came, he was there alone. (Matthew 14:23)

> One of those days Jesus went out to a mountainside to pray, and spent the night praying to God. (Luke 6:12)

> Going a little farther, he fell with his face to the ground and prayed. (Matthew 26:39)

Abraham prayed. Rachel prayed. Moses prayed. Joseph prayed. Joshua prayed. Elijah prayed. Elisha prayed. Gideon prayed. Hannah prayed. Samuel prayed. David prayed. Mary prayed. Peter prayed. John prayed. Paul prayed. Throughout history God has met with people who prayed to Him. Do you long to go and meet with Him? Go to a praying place and enter into His presence. He has invited us to come. If we do not go, we will miss the blessing He will freely give.

Though prayer came naturally to Jesus, prayer is not the natural disposition of our temperament. It is a learned thing, improved by repetition, and understood by the passage of time. The experience of making petitions and receiving answers moves the reality of prayer from abstract to concrete.

OUR SILHOUETTE

How can we become like Jesus in praying? How can we take on His same attitude and temperament? The call on the saint is to pray the way Jesus prayed. We become like Him when we "pray in the Spirit on all occasions with all kinds of prayers and requests."

First, meditate on the attributes of God. Second, as the attributes of God draw attention to your own weakness and sin, confess all known sins. Ask God to search you and point out any blind spots and then confess them, too. Third, ask God to control and empower you with His Holy Spirit. Now, you are in the Spirit.

What next? "Pray in the Spirit on all occasions with all kinds of prayers and requests.... Always keep on praying for all the saints" (Ephesians 6:8). Pray on all occasions. Pray without ceasing. Pray in affliction. Pray with thanksgiving. Pray for the salvation of others. Pray for the physical needs of others. Pray with your spirit and your mind. Pray for those who will someday cry at your funeral. Pray for yourself. Pray in the Holy Spirit. And when you are weak and don't know how to pray, "the Spirit himself intercedes for us with groans that words cannot express" (Romans 8:26).

Who do you talk to when you are mulling over a problem or daydreaming away the time? If you find yourself talking to yourself, stop. Talk it over with the Lord instead. Let Him be your soul mate. Anytime you catch yourself talking to yourself, redirect the conversation to God. That's what it means to pray without ceasing.

The Lord saves our prayers. In heaven are "golden bowls full of incense, which are the prayers of the saints" (Revelation 5:8). He loves prayer, and He loves the one who prays. He loves to answer prayer in ways that contribute to His plan and purpose.

But most of all, Jesus loves to have communion with us through prayer. The natural disposition of Jesus is to pray. He continues to intercede for us: "He always lives to intercede for them" (Hebrews 7:25).

Though not our natural disposition, if we superimpose ourselves over the silhouette of Jesus, prayer can become our first disposition. Is prayer your first disposition, or a hidden asset?

I SURRENDER

Lord Jesus, I want to be like You in prayer. I confess that the natural disposition of my temperament is to rely on my own ingenuity and talent. Forgive me for not being like You in prayer. I had not considered how much You personally love prayer, how much the Bible heroes loved prayer, and how prayer is the hidden asset on my spiritual balance sheet. Teach me to pray. Amen.

THIRTY-ONE

Prayer: Praying for the Inarticulate Need

The Spirit helps us in our weakness. We do not know what we ought to pray, but the Spirit himself intercedes for us with groans that words cannot express.

Romans 8:26

Over a period of several years I witnessed to a prominent executive. One day he invited me to lunch. He offered no agenda, and so I didn't ask for one.

After briefly covering news, sports, and weather, I asked him how things were going on his spiritual pilgrimage. I watched as deep-felt emotions welled up from the center of his soul, but he could not express them. Instead, moisture formed in the corners of reddening eyes. He knew his need was spiritual—that's why we were having lunch together—yet his thoughts remained inarticulate.

Do you ever have difficulty finding words to express your deepest thoughts? Everyone has deep reflections, but sometimes we don't command the language to express them verbally. Passion floods our emotions, but it comes in vague, inexpressible, muddled waves of incomprehensible thought. Words escape us. Our mouths open, but no words come out. The secrets of our hearts remain locked up.

This man wanted to say something to God, but he didn't know where to begin. Further discussion revealed that thirty years had passed since he last prayed to God. When he had been a boy of twelve, his younger, eight-year-old brother contracted a virus and became deathly ill.

He prayed, "God, please, please make my little brother get well." His brother died, and he had cried and cried and cried. He wept bitterly in following years, but the tears did not expunge his bitterness. "Why, God, why? Why didn't you answer my prayer?"

Then he turned to me and said, "I want to believe, but I was so hurt that God didn't spare my brother, I haven't spoken to Him since. Now I want to, but I don't know how—I don't know where to begin."

Have you ever been so overwhelmed by life that you didn't even know where to begin praying? During the hard days—the days when troubles without number overtake us—all our Lord asks is that we come to Him. He makes no demands upon us. Rather, in His compassion, mercy, and gentle loving-kindness He entreats: "'Come to me, all you who are weary and burdened, and I will give you rest'" (Matthew 11:28).

But what do we say to Him? If you say nothing at all, He will understand our need perfectly. The inarticulate need that is still unknown to us is transparent to the Lord. We have scales over our eyes, but the living Lord knows what we need before we even ask. How does that work? When you are too weak to pray—too inarticulate—the Holy Spirit will pray for you. "We do not know what we ought to pray, but the Spirit himself intercedes for us with groans that words cannot express" (Romans 8:26).

When you are too weak to pray, Jesus will pray for you, too. "Christ Jesus, who died . . . is at the right hand of God and is also interceding for us" (Romans 8:34).

Can you imagine any prayer partners with better credentials? The Holy Spirit and Jesus Christ both intercede for you in prayer. Not only so, but their prayers are made in accordance with God's will for you. "The Spirit intercedes for the saints in accordance with God's will" (Romans 8:27).

You have no unknown needs. The Father knows everything about you. "'For your Father knows what you need before you ask him'" (Matthew 6:8). The Father knows, and the Holy Spirit intercedes for you, and Jesus intercedes for you. The loving, living God is working out the purpose of His will in you.

There will be days when—depressed, discouraged, disheartened—you will go home early thinking, "I am so weary that I just don't know how I can go on for one more day." When life's breakers crash down around you, how should you pray? Should you ask God for specifics? Yes, certainly, but what about those times when our problems are so overwhelming that we don't even know where to begin?

Begin where you are. Come to Jesus. He will give you rest. Pray to the Father. Don't be concerned if words don't come. The Spirit Himself will intercede for you with groans that words cannot express. And Jesus, seated next to the Father, will also implore the Lord for your unknown need. Whatever it is. However big it is.

When the weariness of the world wears you down, go to your praying place. The Spirit will meet you there. Jesus will meet you there. They will take you to the Father.

And in the dawn of tomorrow, a new day will bring renewed hope. The weariness will be replaced by the strength for another day. "Weeping may remain for a night, but rejoicing comes in the morning" (Psalm 30:5). In due time He will restore you to the joy of your salvation. In the meantime, let the Spirit and the Lord Jesus carry the load for you in prayer.

The man I lunched with still hasn't negotiated the terms of surrender with Christ. He still wallows in bitterness. With great hope I still pray he will one day soon lower his head and say, "Dear God, I don't know quite where to begin but, Lord, I need You...."

Life is scary. With my middle aged-ness has come the increasing awareness of how little control I have, and have had, over my affairs. Though I often remember a sense of power and autonomy surging through my mind, I can look back and confess that I have really had very little to do with what has happened in my life. I think I will pray more, especially when I don't know where to begin.

I SURRENDER

Dear Lord, there are times when I simply have no idea about how to pray. I want to speak with You, but I don't know where to begin; the right words elude me. Life is scary sometimes. My problems seem overwhelming sometimes. I come to You, Lord Jesus, seeking rest for my weary soul. I surrender my plans to You. I need You. Revive my soul with hope. Heal my brokenness. Amen.

THIRTY-TWO

Prayer: The Method of Prayer

*"I tell you the truth, if you have faith and do not doubt
... you can say to this mountain, 'Go, throw yourself
into the sea,' and it will be done. If you believe, you will
receive whatever you ask for in prayer."*

Matthew 21:21–22

You and I will never have the faith that a mountain can
be hurled into the sea. It is a logical impossibility. No
rational man can honestly believe it could happen. And
so it will never happen, because it is not possible for a
man to have *true* faith *without* doubt that a mountain will
throw itself into the sea. If that level of faith were possible then it could happen, but it isn't, so it doesn't.

Yet, you have seen a jetty jutting half a mile out into
the ocean. The violent surf crashes against huge boulders
piled on each other to subdue the encroaching sea.
Whereas no man may ever have the faith to believe a
whole mountain can throw itself into the sea, many have
had enough faith to believe they could blast a mountain
into a heap of rubble with dynamite, and then haul it off

in rail cars and trucks—boulder by boulder—to build a jetty into the sea.

Many men have moved mountains. And each mountain ever so moved resulted from someone having the faith that they could move a mountain into the sea.

What is your mountain? What perplexing problem rises up like an immovable mountain between you and God? Faith can and will move it, though maybe through the back-breaking work that shatters it into smaller stones instead of a mountain-moving miracle. Is a mountain moved by perseverance any less moved than one moved by a miracle? In either case, faith moved the mountain.

No area of Christian life is more confusing than how to pray and what to expect as the result. Surely, you and I have prayed in faith for many requests which God did not grant. Was Jesus, then, not telling the truth? I don't think so. Was He trying to make another point in the passage? I don't think so again. How does prayer actually work?

The method of prayer breaks simply into two parts: God's part and our part.

OUR PART

Our part in prayer is to believe. That's it. Whatever need or desire we have, we bring it to Christ in faith, believing that *He is able*.

We don't have to believe that God *will* do a certain thing, but that God *can* do a certain thing. In other words, faith is not believing that God will do what you request, but that He can if it is in His will.

GOD'S PART

God's part in prayer is to do whatever He wants. "This is the confidence we have in approaching God: that if we ask anything according to his will, he hears us. And if we know that he hears us—whatever we ask—we know that we have what we asked of him" (1 John 5:14–15).

God hears every prayer offered according to His will. We, then, can pray two kinds of prayers: prayers that agree with God's will and prayers that don't agree with God's will. The ones that agree He hears, and He enlarges our faith from *God can* to *God will*.

Not only does He hear prayers when we ask according to His will, what He hears He does. "Whatever we ask—we know that we have what we asked of him" (v.15).

Which prayers are according to God's will? From the negative angle, since our part is to pray in faith and not doubt, then we can know that a doubting prayer will not be heard. It clearly is God's will for us to pray in faith. An undoubting prayer is made according to God's will.

Prayer without doubt is a condition to being heard but not the only condition. The second condition is that our prayer be according to His will. We can know that we pray in faith not doubting, but only God knows if our prayer is according to His will.

THE BOTTOM LINE

Quite simply, the prayer offered in faith (our part) which is according to the will of God will be heard, and what He hears He does (God's part).

So we pray in faith, not doubting, but not knowing if it is His will. He, on the other end, hears what is prayed *in faith* and *according to His will*—and does it.

Prayer includes our part—to believe, and God's part—to do whatever He wants.

What has tested your faith? What prayer have you uttered that has gone unanswered, even though you prayed in absolute faith that God is able? Is God able? Yes He is. Is God willing? If your prayer is unanswered He has not been willing. But do not become weary in your prayer of faith, for what God has not yet done may still be in His will. It may yet come to pass.

The bottom line is this: Never give up. Let your faith rise as a pleasing fragrance mixed with the tears of your unanswered prayer. His will for you presently is that you persevere in faith, before He yet answers your prayer.

I SURRENDER

God, I have been confused about how to pray and what to expect as the result. I thought I must believe that You *will* answer my prayer, not that You *can* answer my prayer if it is according to Your will. Help me to understand the difference between my part and Your part in my prayers. Remotivate me to surrender to a life characterized by expectant, joyful prayers offered in faith. Give me the faith to move my mountain. Amen.

THIRTY-THREE

Prayer: How Prayer Reflects Our Spiritual Phase

"To him who sits on the throne and to the Lamb be praise and honor and glory and power, for ever and ever!"

Revelation 5:13

Let's be honest. When the bills are stacking up and the customers (or kids) are complaining, it's a bit difficult to pray prayers of deeply felt gratitude and adoration to God. Yet, our ultimate destiny in heaven is just that: "Then I heard every creature in heaven and on earth and under the sea, and all that is in them, singing: 'To him who sits on the throne and to the Lamb be praise and honor and glory and power, for ever and ever!'"

One obvious question is, of course, how are we to pray in the meantime? And why do more mature Christians seem to pray differently than we do?

Our prayers reflect the state or condition of our spirit. They are a proxy statement for the predisposition of our mind. The tendencies of our prayers reflect which phase of spiritual life we occupy. Are your prayers along the line, "Lord, give me . . . ?" Or is the tenor of your prayers more, "Lord, make me . . . ?" Or do your prayers tend to come out, "Lord, thank you . . . ?" These three approaches to prayer provide the essential clue to which phase of spiritual life we are in.

In our maturing as a Christian we pass through three distinct phases. What are they? And how do they manifest in our prayer life?

THE SPIRIT OF NEED

We are needy people. When God found us we were consumed with needs: relational, emotional, financial, moral, psychological, and spiritual needs. We are needy because we are unable to manage our lives without God's wisdom and guidance.

It seems quite natural, then, that until our temporal lives begin to straighten out, temporal needs would preoccupy our early prayers. The distinctive of our prayers in this first phase of our spiritual life is that they are *prayers of petition*. "Lord, give me. . . ." We are babes in Christ.

But life is not static, and God does not leave us alone. We improve. Over a period of years, God begins to solve the residue of problems lingering from the old pagan life. Balance and order come.

Slowly, the selfishness of our prayers occurs to us. Our lives really were broken, and we desperately needed help. But daylight appears, there is light at the end of the tunnel of our temporal needs, and we realize all our prayers have focused only on needs.

On that day, when we are struck by how one-dimensional our prayers have been, we awaken to a second phase of spirit.

THE SPIRIT OF SURRENDER

After ten or twelve years of praying for myself and others, the reality that God actually answers specific prayers *specifically* began to dawn on me. Not overnight, but slowly, the truth of it all began to move from abstract to personal. I *saw* God answer my prayers. I *heard* of God answering my prayers. I *experienced* God answering my prayers, and the abstractness of it all began to fall away like huge chunks of ice from a thawing iceberg plunging into the sea.

At the same time, the shallowness of "Give me, give me, gimme" started to grate on my spiritual sensibilities. Is there not more to prayer than needs?

When once we see the faithfulness of God to care for us, we want to learn how to follow Him. We come to that point where we want to surrender the silliness of our own ideas to the way of the Lord. Instead of praying, "Lord, give me," we start praying, "Lord, make me." Surrendering to the will of God becomes pre-eminent in our thinking.

During this spiritual phase our prayers become *prayers to discern the will of God*, how to live more Christianly day-by-day. We still have needs, and those prayers continue, but seeking the will of God and to be made over in the image of His Son occupies center stage.

God grinds and chips and polishes the character of His disciple during the second phase of pilgrimage and puts him into useful service. Our ambition is to negotiate the terms of surrender to His will. Eventually we come upon the third phase.

THE SPIRIT OF GRATITUDE

The surrendered saint survives the crucibles in which full abandon and total submission are learned. The symptoms of the unsurrendered life have almost disappeared—impure thoughts, selfish ambition, wrong motives, negative attitudes. They always lurk as temptations, but they are not as alluring as they once were. This person graduates to a grateful heart.

The Christian with the spirit of gratitude finds his prayers become *prayers of praise, adoration, and thanksgiving to God.* "Lord, thank you." He rests on the utter dependability of God to accomplish everything He promises, whether a blessing or a threat against sin. It is the most sublime state: a full, total, complete, unequivocal, no retreat, no regrets surrender to Christ. Gladness of heart occupies his thoughts, regardless of circumstantial strains. Beams of gratitude continually shine warmth on the personal relationship with Christ.

The grateful saint still prays for needs and still seeks the will of God, but a spirit of gratitude overarches every utterance to God. Praise and adoration accompany every visit to the throne of grace.

What is the state of your spirit? Which phase are you in? God has ordained the phase of spiritual pilgrimage you are in, but you may eagerly desire a deeper life. Go farther.

The highest calling in prayer is the adoration of God. "'To him who sits on the throne and to the Lamb be praise and honor and glory and power, for ever and ever!'" One day this will be our exclusive prayer. In the meantime, as you pray, "Lord, give me," and "Lord, make me," also pray, "Lord, thank you."

I SURRENDER

Lord, I acknowledge I demonstrate a spirit of need more than of surrender or gratitude in my prayers. I ask You to help me straighten out my life. Enable me to negotiate the terms of a full surrender to You. Grant me a spirit of gratitude. Help me to lead a fully surrendered life, and to offer prayers which express my deep gratitude to You for saving me from my sins.

To Him who sits on the throne and to the Lamb be praise and honor and glory and power, for ever and ever! Amen.

THIRTY-FOUR

The Mind: Above All Else

Above all else, guard your heart, for it is the wellspring of life.

Proverbs 4:23

Recently I have been severely shaken by the number of men and women I know who have stopped following Christ. These are not merely people who tried Christianity for a few weeks or months and then whisked off like a fickle hummingbird darting from one spring flower to the next in search of sweeter nectar. I'm speaking of committed, spiritual people who, after they tasted and saw that the Lord is good for a decade or more, slowly drifted away.

Solomon fit that description. He trusted God to be his strength, his wisdom, and his refuge. He enjoyed the fruit of God's blessings. But he forgot to fear God. He forgot to remain obedient. He forgot to guard his mind.

Solomon's lifeview and worldview drifted from the rock-solid absolutes of Scripture to the world of feelings, to the secular lifeview and worldview of the pagans around him. He forgot to guard his heart. From the wisest man to ever walk the face of the earth to the most disillusioned, Solomon became one of history's most pathetic characters.

A VOICE FROM THE PAST

I wonder how many of the deceased long to call back from their death-chambers and plead with us to live differently. God afforded Solomon such an opportunity. The author of many proverbs, the echo of his voice reverberates down through the ages with lessons from his own indiscretions, ones that left him in tortured, twisted pain. He says, "Above all else, guard your heart, for it is the wellspring of life" (Proverbs 4:23).

Solomon knew that the "place" the enemy would attack would be the heart (mind). The evil one plots to conform your mind to the pattern of this world's view. "See to it that no one takes you captive through hollow and deceptive philosophy" (Colossians 2:8). The Christian must struggle to survive in a non-Christian world. More people desire for you to conform to pagan ways than would see you soar on wings like eagles.

The Christian life and worldview depends upon the Word of God for its moral framework. The secular life and worldview depends upon feelings and empirical demonstration for its moral bearings. The pathetic reality is that our friends who are not Christian always hit the wall. But why is it that countless Christians also hit the wall?

A group of twenty-five Christian men revealed that only five of them were maintaining the purity of their marriages. How can this be? When we live by our feelings, when we pick and choose among the benefits of a secular life, we inevitably weaken our resistance to its temptations. We forget to guard our minds.

Christians can live by the Spirit, or succumb to the sinful nature. To live by the Spirit is not nearly the same as living by feelings. To live by feelings means you decide what is best for your life on the shifting sands of your human understanding. To live by the Spirit means that you go to the Word of God and build a course of action on a firm foundation of rock.

WEAPONRY

The Word assists us for both offense and defense. The sword of the Spirit—the Word of God—is an offensive weapon. "Take ... the sword of the Spirit, which is the word of God" (Ephesians 6:17). Anything we want which conflicts with Scripture is a desire of the sinful nature, and all such feelings are unreliable. We can pierce and slay those desires to know where they will lead with the "sword of the Spirit." Don't guard your feelings, guard your heart, and guard it with the Word.

The Word also functions for defense, to guard our minds. "Take the helmet of salvation ... which is the word of God" (Ephesians 6:17). The helmet guards the head; salvation takes place in the mind. Eternal defeat takes place in the mind, too. In the same way a helmet saves the head from mortal wounds, the Word of God saves the mind from Satan's infinite wound.

Solomon knew his own mind had been left unguarded. He languished in the smoldering ashes of a ruined life. He warns us from his grave. Have you been guarding your heart? Or do you live by your feelings? How have you left your heart unguarded? Pity the pathetic people who leave their minds unguarded, for many of them will stop following Christ.

Have you surrendered your mind to the right life and worldview? If you have left your heart unguarded, hurry and go post a sentinel at the gate to your mind. "Above all else, guard your heart, for it is the wellspring of life."

I SURRENDER

Father, I have left no sentinel posted to guard my heart. My mind has drifted toward a secular life and worldview. The Word of God has not been my defense. The Word of God has not been my offense. I am gripped by these haunting words called out from Solomon's grave. Enable me to guard my heart, above all else. Amen.

THIRTY-FIVE

Quiet Time:
Meeting with God

But if from there you seek the Lord your God, you will find him if you look for him with all your heart and with all your soul.

Deuteronomy 4:29

The alarm didn't go off. The kids rolled out of bed in a cranky mood. The toaster burned breakfast. Someone forgot to plug in the iron. The neighbor's dog chewed up the newspaper again. It's raining. It's your day to car pool, and the car engine won't start.

When the Bible teacher says, "and the most important part of the day is a quiet time," it sounds good, real good. But as the momentary and immediate problems of everyday life set in, making the transition is no easy task. Why is a quiet time so important? What is supposed to happen there? And how does one pull it off?

The quiet time often becomes a hollow convention of religious structure, instead of a holy meeting with the personal Christ. We read a verse or two of Bible, pray a little prayer and—oops! It's 7:30. Amen, and off to work again. That's one more item checked off the daily to-do list, another installment payment on a spiritual insurance policy.

Our quiet times often become yet another perfunctory duty of the Christian life, another activity to verify our Christianity to ourselves. When once this happens, the quiet time has become secularized. We cannot apply worldly methods to spiritual needs.

We are too busy. The suffocating pace of secular society subtly strangles our personal devotions. We must come apart to meet with the Lord. But, it seems we can barely function without the dull drone of a radio or a television in the background

Some of us have forgotten *why* we take time, and with *Whom* we spend it. Instead of thinking of devotions in terms of what we want from God, perhaps some of us need to re-evaluate. Let us go and meet with God and humbly quiet ourselves before the throne of His grace. Leave the religious party horns and hats to others.

A great tragedy of our era is that only ten percent of Americans read their Bibles daily, according to a 1986 Gallup poll. A far greater tragedy is that many of us who do read them do so out of a sense of duty and without much joy. Yet the Word is everything to the life of a Christian.

There is an order to life, a continuity, a progression. It is from *faith* to *obedience*, not from obedience to faith. Paul's mission was to call people "to the obedience that comes from faith" (Romans 1:5). And how do we acquire the bedrock of faith? We meet with God. "Faith comes from hearing the message, and the message is heard through the word of Christ" (Romans 10:17). Do you meet with and listen to God?

There is such a thing as a dry quiet time. When we walk upon deserts of disobedience, our thirst for God goes unmet. When we are caught up in rat race we must live out of the reserves. Yet our loving Father entreats us to come, no matter how far we have strayed. "But if from there you seek the Lord your God, you will find him if you look for him with all your heart and with all your soul" (Deuteronomy 4:29).

Are you depending upon the religious structure of your life instead of your personal relationship with Him? Go and meet with God. You will find Him "if you look for him with all your heart and with all your soul."

Have you devoted yourself to looking for Him with all your heart and all your soul? Or are your quiet times like the hot dry breath of a desert wind? Go and meet with God. Do the first thing first. His breath is cool and refreshing. It is the Holy Spirit who will revive you.

I SURRENDER

Holy Father, I humble myself before You. I have trivialized the time I spend with You. The plain truth is that I have made it into a duty and an obligation. And I have let myself become very busy. Lord, I surrender my time to You. I ask You to grant me the grace to put first things first. I want to meet with You. I want You to be Lord. I want to re-Christianize my personal devotions. Let the breath of Your Spirit revive my personal relationship with You in quiet times. Amen.

THIRTY-SIX

Scripture: Gaining Spiritual Weight

> *Like newborn babies, crave pure spiritual milk, so that by it you may grow up in your salvation, now that you have tasted that the Lord is good.*
>
> 1 Peter 2:2–3

My dad was my hero. I remember his strong muscular physique, and how I wanted to grow up to be exactly like him in every way.

I was puny—the classic ninety-seven-pound weakling. So as a young ten-year-old boy I fell hook, line, and sinker for the "Charles Atlas" ads that promised all us little boys that we could be titans of toughness, gain those precious pounds, and never again have big-mouthed bullies kick sand on us. They could help make me strong, just like dad!

If someone wants to gain five pounds, he doesn't eat five pounds of food and instantly register five pounds at the scales. Instead, he eats five pounds of food and incrementally gains an ounce or two. Then he eats another five pounds of food and gains another few ounces, and so on.

Obviously, the energy needed for the daily press burns up most of our daily food intake.

When someone wants to gain spiritual weight they don't read five pounds of Bible and gain five pounds of spiritual weight. Rather, he studies the Scriptures for an hour or so and is fortunate to gain one or two spiritual insights to add to his spiritual weight.

Most of the five pounds of Bible we might devour during our personal devotions gets burned up on that day's challenges or quickly forgotten, and we add only an ounce or two of new spiritual bulk.

The Scriptures are similar to the most delicious, well-balanced meal you have ever eaten, one you will often remember and hope to repeat—"now that you have tasted that the Lord is good." What brings us back to the Lord's table? We want to add to our spiritual weight. We want food that lasts, that adds precious ounces of spiritual wisdom and truth. We must consume much to retain little, so we come again and again each day. Do not fast from the Scriptures, or you will grow weak. Nourish your soul daily. Drink of the Word of God. Eat of it, and add weight to your beliefs.

We live in a Christianized age, but an age of spiritual malnutrition. We are heavyweights when it comes to spiritual talk, but desperately lightweight in our behavior. Have you unwittingly been on a spiritual fast? Are you weak from abstaining from "pure spiritual milk"? Have you made the error of thinking five pounds of Bible will add five pounds of spiritual weight?

If anything is true, it is that for our spirit and soul to grow we must drink daily from His cup and eat daily of His body. We must be regular—daily—in our intake of spiritual food. We need a balanced spiritual diet. Too much of one and too little of another will lead to spiritual malnutrition.

Do you want to be spiritually healthy? Do you want to "grow up in your salvation"? Then crave pure spiritual food; eat and drink of it. Desire the Word to nourish your soul more than food and drink for your body. "'Do not worry about your life, what you will eat or drink.... Is not life more important than food?'" (Matthew 6:25).

To gain an ounce of spiritual weight you must take on five pounds of spiritual food, daily, in balanced proportions. Most of what you consume will be burned up as spiritual energy for that day. Linger at the table, feasting on His pure food, consuming more than a day's supply, and add an ounce or two to your spiritual weight. This is the prerequisite step to growing up in your salvation. Insufficient intake means insufficient growth.

Do you want to grow up to be like your Father? If you partake daily at His table, you will grow up to be like Him.

I SURRENDER

Dear Father, I yearn to add spiritual weight to my life. I have been living out of the reserves. I will spend more time consuming Your Word. Help me to linger at Your table. I will crave a balanced spiritual diet. I have tasted and know that the Lord is good. Amen.

PART SEVEN

Responding to the Struggles of Daily Life

Once we have saving faith, what kind of faith helps us overcome the struggles of daily life? It is persevering faith, which is the signature of the surrendered life.

THIRTY-SEVEN

Grace: Living Worthy of Our Calling

I urge you to live a life worthy of the calling you have received.

Ephesians 4:1

A young man returned from the war in Vietnam. The destruction he witnessed left him disturbed, somehow unbalanced. He could not shake the aftermath of the depraved images he had observed firsthand. He had participated in the confusing ways of this broken world, and he despaired of the evil which men do to each other.

Not long after his return stateside, he received the calling to trust Christ for his salvation—a call to which he said yes. As he prayed "Lord Jesus, I need You," his body began to twitch and tremble uncontrollably. He had been born, now he was born again. The instability of his disturbed world was replaced by the stability of the kingdom of God.

Over the next several years, he struggled to live a life worthy of the calling he had received, but he did not. The psychological trauma of Vietnam haunted him; people strained his edgy temperament. Eventually he became a commercial fisherman, finding solace in the lonely life of the sea.

Years later we saw each other again, and I asked him how things were going on his spiritual pilgrimage. "Well, I still believe," came his reply. "but it's really hard for me."

One morning three months later I received a phone call. After returning from two weeks at sea, this young man followed his weathered, crusty comrades to the local tavern. He soon passed out. His mates grabbed his arms and legs and carried his limp, languid body into the back room and flopped him like a frumpy, oversized rag doll onto the cold, bare floor. Even though he was turning blue, they turned and walked away. He never regained consciousness. Several hours later he was found dead from a drug and alcohol overdose. He was my younger brother.

Not everyone has the strength of courage and character to live a life worthy of the calling they have received. To live up to our calling is itself a gift from God. "But to each one of us grace has been given as Christ apportioned it" (Ephesians 4:7). Some of us are impeded from living up to Christ. It may be a troubled childhood, a tough marriage, difficult children, or, like my brother, you may have seen too much evil.

Apply Your Grace

If Christ has apportioned you with enough grace to live a life worthy of the calling you received, are you applying it? If not, should He let you keep it? Or should He take it away and give it to someone who will make full use of it? Many Christians under-apply their grace. It is such a waste.

If you are living a life worthy of the calling you received, how do you treat your weaker brother? Do you look on in disgust at your brother who can't quite seem to get his act together? Does your mind get stuck thinking about how weak he is? Pray for him, that God's grace to him may increase. Fall to your face and implore God to have mercy on your weaker brother or sister with tears of remorse. Thank Him with tears of gratitude that He has mercifully given you so much grace. Why should it be the other person and not you that is weak? There is no reason except the grace Christ has apportioned to you at His sole discretion. "But for the grace of God, there go I."

"Be completely humble and gentle; be patient, bearing with one another in love" (Ephesians 4:2). "Accept him whose faith is weak, without passing judgment on disputable matters" (Romans 14:1).

Every Christian is one for whom Christ died. If Jesus thought that person was worth dying for, why do you despise him? "You, then, why do you judge your brother? Or why do you look down on your brother? For we will all stand before God's judgment seat" (Romans 14:10).

Let us, therefore, concentrate on living up to the calling we have received. Part of our calling is to bear with our weaker brothers, to not revel in the smug satisfaction that we overcome but they don't. If we overcome, it is because of the grace apportioned to us. And if we ourselves are not living a life worthy of our calling, then ask for more grace. Work out your salvation with fear and trembling, but know that the strength of courage and character to do so comes from the grace apportioned to you.

I SURRENDER

Dear God, I am ashamed of the ways I have thought of and treated my weaker brothers and sisters. I have looked down on them, but now I see how it is my own weakness. Give the one I have disdained more grace. I praise and thank You for the grace You have apportioned to me, Lord Jesus. God, where I am the weaker one, I pray that You would have mercy and compassion on me and grant me more grace that I may live a life worthy of the calling I have received. Amen.

THIRTY-EIGHT

Perseverance: The Need for Persevering Faith

You need to persevere so that when you have done the will of God, you will receive what he has promised.

Hebrews 10:36

Have you ever known a time when you thought you would die if the Lord did not give you His touch? A time when no friend could comfort you? When you could see no way out? When your circumstances gave new meaning to the word bleak?

Bart decided to ask God to shape his character. He surrendered his own will to the will of God. At the time, Bart's business floundered on the verge of failure. "Should I throw in the towel, or keep trying to hang on?" Bart wondered.

God replies, "You need to persevere." After we have done the will of God, then we will receive our reward. God's will is for us to demonstrate to a hurting world how wonderfully His power can work within the person who perseveres.

Certainly, there are days when we feel like we will die, or maybe even wished we could, but we keep going. Why?

Why do we keep going? Because *when* we have done the will of God, we *will* receive what He has promised.

Will persevering guarantee we will succeed in the worldly sense of success? Is that what He has promised? Does it mean we will not go out of business if we hang on? No, but we can state emphatically that if we don't persevere we will not succeed in any sense. Not persevering guarantees we will fail.

What exactly is it, then, that He has promised? Jesus said, "'Whoever does God's will is my brother and sister and mother'"(Mark 3:35). When you have persevered, you become transformed into part of the family of Christ. You become His friend, and He prays for you in the presence of the Father.

Beyond succeeding in a worldly sense, though, God wants our character to succeed more than our circumstances to succeed. He will adjust our circumstances in such a way that our character eventually succeeds, that is His highest aim, His will.

To receive this kingdom of God is our highest aim. We want to be part of the world that is coming, not part of the world that is going. So we must conclude we want to do the will of God. But is our life and lifestyle really an expression of that will?

WHAT TURNS US FROM THE WILL OF GOD?

When prosperity surrounds a man too long, his own self-will begins to growl within him like the deep rumblings of an inactive volcano just before it once again erupts. Though now dormant, its rugged features remind us of the violent eruptions of which it is capable. In the same way, we walk calmly with Christ, but our features give us away. Tiny, barely visible rivulets of cooled-down pride give us away and betray our past. Our pride is not gone, only dormant. Prosperity prompts pride; it reactivates a volcano of self-will, and that person forgets God.

Here is how Moses put it:

> When you have eaten and are satisfied, praise the Lord your God for the good land he has given you. Be careful that you do not forget the Lord your God, failing to observe his commands, his laws and his decrees.... Otherwise ... your heart will become proud and you will forget the Lord your God. (Deuteronomy 8:10–14)

Suffering is not far behind.

WHAT TURNS US BACK TO THE WILL OF GOD?

When Christians suffer, their agony grinds out of them the desire to have a will of their own apart from the will of God. Suffering can produce a good result: perseverance. When you do persevere, you will receive what was promised—you will become His brother. You will be like Him. He will be able to use your life to strengthen other broken people. Your sympathy will become empathy.

And because you persevered, because you received what was promised, because you have no will of your own, because you are the brother—the sister—of Jesus, you will become the expression of Christ's compassion to your brother on earth. People will ask if they can speak privately with you so they can weep and pour out their desperation to you.

So why persevere? He has promised the joy of being Christ's brother and administering the gospel of His compassion. D. L. Moody was fond of saying, "The reward of service is more service." Christ's reward for you is *useful* service, service that lasts.

I Surrender

Lord Jesus, help me to persevere. Sometimes I feel like giving up. I vacillate between Your will and my own, between prosperity and suffering. Stabilize me. Give me the strength to persevere, and let me receive the reward You have promised. Amen.

THIRTY-NINE

Faith: Living by Faith

We live by faith, not by sight.

2 Corinthians 5:7

Last year was a long year for me. The tides ebbed. When the tides of life are rising, singing silent praises to God comes easily. It is not difficult to be thankful when God is blessing. For years my tides rose, the circumstances continually improved. Not that hard times never stayed out of the picture, but they were manageable hard times—common sense and hard work could solve the problems.

Every rising tide eventually retreats to the sea. Whether it's the high winds of financial or family disaster, the stormy seas of broken relationships, or the washed away beaches of illness or death—we all live in circumstances that rise and fall like the tides. Inevitably, almost predictably, come the changes.

TIME TO TAKE A VACATION

No matter how spiritual we are, we all expend our physical energies on our problems, and we need rest not only for our souls but for our minds and bodies.

So I anticipated our summer vacation to the mountains for months on end. The only prerequisite I had established in my mind for this retreat from reality was that the home we rent have a mountain view.

Our arrival at our vacation escape was the equivalent to the first time I spotted my high school sweetheart holding hands with my best friend. Not only did we not have a mountain view, as near I as could tell, our cubbyhole marked the nadir of the valley.

There's more. The furnishings looked like they had been discarded along a roadside, loaded in a pick-up truck, and carted to this place. This nook was so tiny I couldn't negotiate our luggage up the stairs. A rancid odor hung like a muggy fog.

I fell into a state of despair, alternating between moody brooding and raging anger. Pure chaos rampaged with my emotions.

Oh, I know the arguments. I used them on myself: Think of all the poor people who can't even afford a vacation. Think of all the people with large families who live full-time in houses even smaller. Think of the two-thirds of the world who don't have enough to eat. Think of how quickly your priorities would change if one of the children broke a leg. Think of how ungrateful you are being toward God who, after all, is the final cause of all things.

Somehow these thoughts didn't help. Besides, nobody did break a leg, and I really needed a vacation. Frankly, I didn't want the *rational* man in me to speak. The *emotional* man had the floor, and he wasn't about to give it up.

As humorous as situations like these are in hindsight, and we have all had them, it would be helpful to know how to work through them at the time they occur. What is the proper response?

GOD CAUSES OR ALLOWS

Here is the important point: God is the final cause of all things. He authors every chapter in our lives. He either *causes* or *allows* every tide that rises and falls. That is reality. Even Satan operates under the permission of God (see Job 1:8–12).

We think the issue is how to bring the *rational man*, the *emotional man*, and the *volitional man* back onto an even keel—to reconcile the differences within us, usually by making a change. "I will call the rental agent up and demand a different place, or get our money back." That is not the issue.

The issue is how do we *surrender* to the Holy Spirit *in our circumstances as they exist*. That does not seem rational. What seems rational is, "I worked very hard under very difficult circumstances last year and I deserve to have my money's worth and I shall not settle for less." What we most often want to do is to change our circumstances. God doesn't want to change our circumstances; He wants to change us.

THE EMOTIONS, THE MIND, OR THE WILL?

Most of us have heard that the Christian is not to live by his feelings. True enough. The emotional man is not to be trusted. But I would propose that it is equally true that the Christian is not to depend upon his knowledge. I speak here not of spiritual knowledge but rational knowledge. The Scriptures commend growth in spiritual knowledge. Paul prayed for the brothers in Colosse, "We have not stopped praying for you and asking God to fill you with the knowledge of his will through all spiritual wisdom and understanding" (Colossians 1:9).

The rational man cannot be trusted any more than the emotional man. Merely look at the terrible rational decisions we all make. Nothing is easier than self-deceit. Our best thinking can end in disaster. The rational man would demand a refund. But what does Jesus want to teach us?

The Christian life is to be lived in the will by faith. "The righteous will live by faith" (Romans 1:17). The volitional man decides to live by faith in the Word and not according to the deductions of his intellect. Yes, it is essential to exercise the intellect—most Christians don't do enough thinking. But when rationality clashes with the Word, leave your suspected genius behind. At the end of the day, faith is more important than rationality, and faith always triumphs over circumstances. Leave room in your thinking for spiritual mystery.

Never quit on faith. Some things just take time. As much as I wanted to surrender our vacation woes to the Spirit, the impulses of the old man within me battled against it. And that is precisely why we didn't have a mountain view. Oh, for sure the rental agent misled us. But she was the second cause—God was the first cause. And God knew where my character was weak, where I wasn't willing to fully surrender.

It now occurs to me that you may think this is a silly example, that many more serious situations could better illustrate these points. But let me say that the true disasters of life are often easier to come to terms with than the struggles of the daily grind.

THE MYSTERY OF FAITH

In the final analysis, it is not all that important that you and I understand—see—every detail of our lives, but it is supremely important that by faith we yield control of every detail to the Spirit. A successful Christian life doesn't need the rationality of sight, but it does need the faith of surrender.

Life doesn't seem rational sometimes, but a collage of peculiar mysteries. Our circumstances appear difficult. The logical, rational thing would be to make a change. Look a little longer before you make that change. What is God trying to teach you? Have you surrendered your circumstances to Him?

I SURRENDER

Lord, I confess that I burn up my energies trying to establish order in my life. I have tried to live by sight. Help me to make more allowance for spiritual mystery. Help me to live by faith. I have wanted to change my circumstances. Show me how You want to change my character. Amen.

FORTY

Affliction: When God Is Silent

It is good to wait quietly for the salvation of the Lord.

Lamentations 3:26

Dear Father,

I have raced way ahead of You on a fast track. Striving for the future has consumed my years. In times past my heart bulged with the things of God, but then I became busy, and I have not spent much time with You for quite a while now.

I hit the future I was aiming for. I grabbed for the brass ring and got it. I did it my way. But not only did I do it my way in my career, I also did it my way in the rest of my life, too. I have led a life that is somehow unbalanced. Now, I suspect my life is either at a breaking point, or a turning point.

What I really don't understand though, God, is that I have prayed day-after-day-after-day, and You don't seem to be answering. Why will You not answer me? Have I slipped so far that there is no redemption left for me? I earnestly desire to turn away from the hollow and deceptive philosophies that tripped me up. But how can I do it if You won't answer me?

I don't think I can take the pressure much longer. Everyone wants a piece of me. I have just about completely alienated my family. I am tired. I am worn out. I don't feel like I have the strength to fight back. My emotions are sad. When will You come and save me?

God does not bring affliction upon us willingly. He finds no pleasure in our pain. God is not the root cause of our problems; He is the solution. The reason for many of our afflictions is our disobedience to the will of God—doing our own thing, living by the desires of the sinful nature. The sinful nature leads us into good ideas that are not God ideas. One good idea leads to another, and before long we have wandered away from the Lord.

Though God is not the root cause of our affliction, He is the effective cause. Because our personal relationship with Him is God's highest priority, He invariably afflicts the life of the one who strays. But He never does this willingly, or with enjoyment. "For he does not willingly bring affliction or grief to the children of men" (Lamentations 3:33). His Spirit grieves when we wander, and when He afflicts us, sorrow pierces the heart of God.

The silence of God teaches humility, creates character, and produces perseverance. When a man or woman humbly seeks the mind of God, learning to dwell patiently in the silence, God will revive that soul. He will reveal His love and compassion in the silence. His gentle, quiet Spirit cannot be heard above the roaring rapids of a raging river. He is found beside still waters.

Has God afflicted your life? Are you at a breaking point? Convert it from a breaking point to a turning point. Go seek Him beside still waters. Enter into the silence of God. Wait, and wait patiently, for Him to speak.

Is He silent when you call out? Wait quietly for Him to speak. With the Lord a thousand years is but a day. Here is your encouragement:

> The Lord is good to those whose hope is in him,
>   to the one who seeks him;
> It is good to wait quietly
>   for the salvation of the Lord.
> It is good for a man to bear the yoke
>   while he is young.
> Let him sit alone in silence,
>   for the Lord has laid it on him....
> For men are not cast off by the Lord forever.
> Though he brings grief, he will show compassion,
>   so great is his unfailing love
>
> Lamentations 3:25–32

The normal believer's expectation is that he can live twenty years pursuing the God he wanted, turn to the God who is, and twenty minutes later all the issues will be resolved. That is not how God works.

God's business is to sanctify our lives of every alien thought. When we begin to bring thoughts captive to make them obedient to Christ, we discover that deprogramming from the secular lifeview takes as long as the programming did. It takes as long to abandon to Christ as it did to abandon from Christ.

When you are afflicted and God is silent, it is good to wait quietly for His salvation. Do not give up. He is not on the way, He has already arrived, but you must bear up until He speaks. His silence will teach you. Will you accept His yoke of silence?

The silence of God precedes the outpouring of His compassion. His great love for us is the only reason we are not instantly consumed for our years of self-sufficiency. Surrender your expectations to the silence. Wait for the God who is to speak. You will not be disappointed.

I SURRENDER

Dear God, the God who is, I have struggled in the silence. I has misinterpreted the silence. I have had expectations which are based on my own logic. My afflictions have brought me to the breaking point. I pray You will aid me in making it into a turning point instead. I surrender to the silence. Use the silence to create character, to teach me humility, to produce perseverance in me. Amen.

FORTY-ONE

Belief: Faith and Doubt Together

"I do believe; help me overcome my unbelief!"

Mark 9:24

All that Christ stood for boiled down to this one great theme: Believe. "'Don't be afraid; just believe'" (Mark 5:36). "'Believe that you have received it, and it will be yours'" (Mark 11:24). "'Just believe, and she will be healed'" (Luke 8:50).

All that Christ asks of you and me is simply, "Believe." Over and over and over again, the Lord issues forth His one simple injunction: "Believe." No matter where this bidding is heard, however, there is doubt. Everywhere He went they answered, "But who is this one? Could He be the Christ?"

Let's be honest. It is a hard thing to believe. When you are waiting for the biopsy results, when the car breaks down the same week the refrigerator dies, when the boss hands you a pink slip, doubt is more natural than belief. In fact, if only one characteristic could be used to describe the average response to Jesus, even by those of us who know Him, it would not be belief, but doubt.

This should not strike us as unusual, for the closest associates of Christ struggled with the demon of doubt. They deserted Him in the garden. After the eleven disciples (now deserters) heard of His resurrection, they still doubted. So He came to them and "rebuked them for their lack of faith and their stubborn refusal to believe those who had seen him after he had risen" (Mark 16:14).

In the last scene of the gospels, the eleven disciples gathered at the mountain where Jesus had told them to go. In a few moments, He would charge them with the Great Commission, "'Therefore go and make disciples of all nations'" (Matthew 28:19). They would witness His ascension. But even then, "When they saw him, they worshiped him; *but some doubted*" (Matthew 28:17, emphasis added).

Jesus did not cast the eleven deserters out of the kingdom because they doubted; instead, He rebuked them. He knows our human frailty. He knows when we will doubt before we know it. He knit us together in our mother's womb and has numbered each of our days. He does not reject us because we doubt. Rather, He exhorts us, "'Don't be afraid; just believe.'"

PERCEPTION VERSUS REALITY

The difficulty of belief is the difference between the physical perception and the divine reality. The physical perception is always hopeless—the deformed child, the broken marriage, the money which is lost and gone. A snapshot of the situation is hopeless, but a snapshot is only one frame of a moving picture. A snapshot freezes time and is part of the reality but not all of it. Life is a moving picture. The snapshot is not reality and, taken alone, it is an inaccurate perception.

The divine reality is always hope. The hindrance to our hope is our doubt. Now, faith will not cure every problem that we want cured. But doubt will cure none of them. So it is better to believe and hope in God than to doubt and languish in despair.

The divine plan is concrete. When we believe, we release His power to help us in ways He wants, even longs, to help us. The divine plan is always for the good of those who love Him and are called according to His purpose. It is the ultimate reality.

Are you a doubter? Does your faith wither when the dry winds of fate blow harshly across the landscape of your life? Jesus says, "Don't be afraid; just believe."

TWO KINDS OF BELIEF

There are two kinds of belief. The first is belief to become a Christian, and then there is belief to live by. The great hurdle is the first one. Passing over the first hurdle lands you into an eternal kingdom. But then there are hundreds and thousands of daily living hurdles—marriage conflicts, health problems, career decisions.

The issue for the Christian is this: Did you believe the first time? If you did, then your job is not to make the believe-or-not-believe decision a thousand more times. Your task is to learn the right response based on the fact of your first belief. If you believed, then you became co-heir with Christ to the kingdom of God. Once you first believe, you are eternally connected to the goodness of God. He has good plans for you, plans which go on for ever and ever.

But in the emulsion of daily life, globules of doubt are suspended all around our faith. Jesus said to the father of the demon-possessed boy, "Everything is possible for him who believes" (Mark 9:23). But the father lived in the emulsion of daily life; physical perceptions were suspended all around the divine reality. That is why the father of the boy exclaimed, "I do believe; help me overcome my unbelief!" (v. 24).

What son is it that you are desperate to have the Lord heal? What sorrow languishes in your soul? Can Jesus heal you? Jesus says, yes, "Everything is possible for him who believes."

I SURRENDER

Lord Jesus, I live in the emulsion of daily life, doubting Your power to heal my life. Sometimes I wonder if You are really there. I pray You will remove doubt from my life. Restore the solid belief in my life of the divine reality. Lord, I do believe; help me with my unbelief! Amen.

FORTY-TWO

Temptation: The Purpose for Severe Temptation

Then Jesus was led by the Spirit into the wilderness to be tempted by the devil.

Matthew 4:1

Have you ever wondered where the cliché "wilderness experience" came from? We have all had them. So did Jesus. The Holy Spirit led Jesus into the wilderness to be tempted by Satan. Does that shock your sensibilities? Are you bothered that the Spirit would initiate temptation?

Actually, the Spirit didn't tempt Jesus—Satan did. "For God cannot be tempted by evil, nor does he tempt anyone" (James 1:13). Yet God led Jesus into the wilderness. He leads us into the wilderness. He has important work for you and me, and He must squeeze the cultural Christianity out of us. To do this He sometimes takes us into the wilderness.

For me it was a period of the deepest, darkest sort of agony—cash flow problems, people problems, and few answers. The awesome pressure of my business problems overwhelmed my emotions. Day after dispirited day I would trudge home to my wife and say with tears streaming down my face, "I am so weary. I just don't know how I can go on one more day."

Frankly, the catastrophe was of my own making. I suppose that's the way it is for most of us. It was my own foolish decisions which yielded such a harvest of heartache. Still, the agonizing pain crushed my spirit into dry, powdered dust. As I wandered around in my wilderness, I sensed a wily devil manipulating my emotions, hoping I would fail the test.

THE GOOD SATAN DOES

God uses Satan for good. Can you believe that? Paul received a thorn in the flesh, *a messenger of Satan, to keep him from becoming conceited* (2 Corinthians 12:7). God used Satan to help Paul from becoming conceited—for good.

In the name of Christ, Paul instructed the Church to hand a sinner over to Satan (see 1 Corinthians 5:5). Why? So that his sinful nature would be destroyed—for good. God is in the business of making His saints holy. Incredulous as it may seem, He frequently uses Satan as an instrument for good. That certainly was the case when Jesus was tempted in the wilderness. He qualified Himself for the work of our Savior.

Satan must have God's permission to sift you, to put you under the severe temptation. "'Simon, Simon, Satan has asked to sift you as wheat'" (Luke 22:31). Don't rebel while you wander in your own wilderness experience; let Satan sift you, and you will learn inexplicable truths about yourself. You will grow into an inarticulate, child-like trust in Jesus.

The Holy Spirit who leads us into the wilderness doesn't leave us; He stays there with us. He may be quiet for the moment, but He is always there. In due time the test will pass. "Then the devil left him, and [by the Holy Spirit] angels came and attended him" (Matthew 4:11). Your angels are waiting for His signal. Stand firm and resist.

A SENSE OF PURPOSE

Of what earthly value could your temptation be? What is the purpose for such a severe test? It is not for you alone. It is to prepare you for important work. "'But I have prayed for you, Simon, that your faith may not fail. *And when you have turned back, strengthen your brothers*'" (Luke 22:32, emphasis added).

When you have stood the test, when He brings you out the other side of the wilderness, after the angels have attended you, become food and drink for your brothers. Let them feed off you. Become a proxy for Jesus who was the bread of life.

I SURRENDER

Lord Jesus, the temptations of my life seem severe. Strengthen me with Your Spirit. I see that the tests of my life are not for me only. Help me to be food and drink from whom others can gain strength. Amen.

FORTY-THREE

Temptation: The Flesh or Satan?

For the sinful nature [the flesh] desires what is contrary to the Spirit, and the Spirit what is contrary to the sinful nature.

Galatians 5:17

Our human nature doesn't like to take responsibility for our actions, preferring instead to blame someone else. We look for a scapegoat to impugn for our sinful deeds. "The devil made me do it" is a favorite.

SATAN

We give Satan too much credit. Satan is fallen. He cannot foretell the future. He is limited in time and space—he can only be one place at a time. He is not eternal. He will someday be put to the second death.

It is impossible for Satan to make you sin. Sin is a *choice*. Satan can tempt us, but we decide to sin. "By his own evil desire, he is dragged away and enticed" (James 1:14). Since the devil is unable to make us sin, we need to reconsider blaming him for our wrong choices.

On the other hand, Satan has successfully created an environment that promotes and encourages sin, much like a company which has done a particularly good job promoting its products. But let's give God credit, too. He has created an environment as well, giving us everything we need to overcome temptation and live a life of power, purpose, and meaning.

True, Satan can provoke men to evil, but the man must still choose for himself whether evil will be his trademark. Satan's power can be resisted by any believer with the enabling power of the Holy Spirit with whom every Christian is indwelt.

Satan is less powerful than one "temptee" who relies on the Holy Spirit to resist. For Satan to go up against one surrendered saint filled with the Holy Spirit is like a bantam-weight boxer standing before the explosive fury of a heavyweight champion-of-the-world's knock-out punch. He's going to lose.

THE FLESH

The Spirit doesn't war against Satan; He wars against the flesh. Satan (death) has already been warred against and defeated at the cross. It is our sinful nature that we must each day crucify anew as we take up our cross daily.

There is no way to know, of course, but I suspect most of our sins result from yielding to the flesh, not yielding to Satan. Perhaps his puny demons lurk around, whispering devious deceptions to our feeble flesh, but we have the Spirit's knock-out punch at our eternal disposal. So sin is better blamed on our sinful nature—not Satan.

Satan's real influence doesn't come from his power but from the temporary jurisdiction he has been granted over Earth. He does not, however, have jurisdiction over

Christians. Even in those rare Job-like experiences when Satan personally attacks, God is yet sovereign, and the devil acts only by His permission.

Because the devil has temporary jurisdiction, he has been able to sabotage the world. Satan is much like the capable-but-crooked branch manager who pursued immoral motives, then fled in disgrace, abandoning a strife-torn field office left in shambles. This temporary jurisdiction is like the short term of the dinky little dictator who became president of a tiny outpost country. Satan is but a teetering tyrant whose term is almost up.

The bigger enemy is our flesh. To square off against Satan is easy by comparison. The flesh must be battled daily, even momentarily. That's why the Scriptures say, "For the . . . Spirit [desires] what is contrary to the sinful nature" and *not* "The Spirit desires what is contrary to Satan." That battle against Satan is already won. The ongoing battle is with the flesh.

The solution: Surrender the flesh to the Spirit. And stop blaming Satan for the sins you enjoy. Rather than saying, "The devil made me do it," we should begin to say, "The flesh made me do it."

I SURRENDER

Heavenly Father, I need to take the responsibility for my actions and stop blaming others. I acknowledge that my sinful nature is my downfall, not Satan. I surrender my flesh to the Spirit. Fill me with the power to be led by the Spirit. Amen.

FORTY-FOUR

Encouragement: I Have to Occasionally Remind Myself

And you have forgotten that word of encouragement.

Hebrews 12:5

We all have those days when sadness oozes into our thoughts. Sometimes our problems come in bunches, and our circuit breakers all flip out at the same time. We simply go into overload.

When we have too many things to think about, we often become discouraged about Jesus. Amid the uproar of clanging thoughts competing for the attention of our minds, the spiritual rhythm we had developed dissolves into doubt and fear and discouragement.

We go before the Lord, wondering where He is. "Why have you left me? My heart was filled with the joy of a sweet melody. Everything was in tune, and I was enjoying such sweet fellowship with You, my Lord. Why did it have to stop?" Surely His Word was in our heart like a burning fire. But where is it just now?

When sadness blows my breakers, I like to read the gospel. The reminders come. I sometimes forget these simple truths for a moment. When again I see them, I am deeply encouraged. Hear these words of encouragement:

"For God so loved the world that he gave his one and only Son, that whoever believes in him shall not perish but have eternal life." (John 3:16)

"Heaven and earth will pass away, but my words will never pass away." (Matthew 24:35)

"Take courage! It is I. Don't be afraid." (Matthew 14:27)

"For the Son of Man came to seek and to save what was lost." (Luke 19:10)

"What good will it be for a man if he gains the whole world, yet forfeits his soul? Or what can a man give in exchange for his soul?" (Matthew 16:26)

Here is a trustworthy saying that deserves full acceptance: Christ Jesus came into the world to save sinners.... (1 Timothy 1:15)

... without the shedding of blood there is no forgiveness. (Hebrews 9:22)

"This is my blood of the covenant, which is poured out for many for the forgiveness of sins." (Matthew 26:28)

"But I, when I am lifted up from the earth, will draw all men to myself." (John 12:32)

But Christ has indeed been raised from the dead, the firstfruits of those who have fallen asleep. (1 Corinthians 15:20)

"But from now on, the Son of Man will be seated at the right hand of the mighty God." (Luke 22:69)

"In the same way your Father in heaven is not willing that any of these little ones should be lost." (Matthew 18:14)

"I give them eternal life, and they shall never perish; no one can snatch them out of my hand." (John 10:28)

No, in all these things we are more than conquerors through him who loved us. For I am convinced that neither death nor life, neither angels nor demons, neither the present nor the future, nor any powers, neither height nor depth, nor anything else in all creation, will be able to separate us from the love of God that is in Christ Jesus our Lord. (Romans 8:37–39)

Sometimes I forget these words of encouragement. It is not the mind-bending, intellectually stimulating truths that encourage our downcast spirit. It is the simple truth of the gospel—the everlasting love of the Lord Jesus—that revives our soul. The old gospel—it is the power of God for the salvation of everyone who believes.

I Surrender

Yes, God, I believe. Send it to me again—Your word of encouragement. Once again, I pray that You will fan the flame of Your gift into a roaring fire. Once again, let me say with Jeremiah, "His Word is in my heart like a burning fire, shut up in my bones. I am weary of holding it in; indeed, I cannot" (Jeremiah 20:9). Amen.

FORTY-FIVE

Satan: Defend Yourself

For Satan himself masquerades as an angel of light. It is not surprising, then, if his servants masquerade as servants of righteousness.

2 Corinthians 11:14–15

For decades Russia and the United States each invested billions to develop new offensive weapon systems that the other cannot defend. The objective? Then the opponent must develop a new budget-busting defensive system or risk a devastating first strike.

The strategies for American and Russian defensive systems differ radically. Russia's jewels are all interior, centered in Moscow. America's jewels are scattered all along our coasts. The methods of defense and offense for these two countries are, of necessity, very different.

A retired U.S. Air Force general explained our national defense system to me: the Strategic Triad consists of our bomber force, ICBM's, and submarines. Any one of the three can defend against a nuclear strike, for they are overlapping systems. Why in the world do we need three overlapping systems? Isn't that a waste of tax dollars? Why did we decide to defend ourselves so carefully? And especially when the Russians frequently appear to exhibit such good intentions?

As the general explained, our national defense policy is built on the premise: We defend against *capabilities*, not *intentions*.

The world is full of good intentions. The Christian is called to give the benefit of the doubt, to go as a sheep among wolves, and to be innocent as a dove. Yet the unwary Christian is likely to accept the good intentions of the world and let down his defenses. When he does, the enemy will mount a full-scale attack, penetrating at the point of weakness where you are not prepared to defend.

The Christian must defend against Satan's capabilities, not his good intentions. He comes as an angel of light. He looks for holes in the wall of our strategic defense system. He will attack undefended vulnerabilities, the jewels.

Maybe you have done a good work for the Lord. Satan will remind you of how much you have done for God and tempt you to pride. Or he knows we want to serve the Lord, and he whispers a good idea into your ear, one that would help save the world, but one that would cause you to sacrifice your family.

Satan will send his servants to you with good ideas—righteous ideas. But they will take you away from God ideas, those priorities that God would have you pursue. A good thing is not necessarily a God thing. The only way to know is to pray. Never accept a good thing until you know it is a God thing. Defend yourself against the crafty offense of the evil one.

Satan doesn't come to the Christian and tempt him to transparent evil. To presume Satan will attack us at our strong point defies good sense. No, instead he will tempt us at the weakest point of our defenses, where we have forgotten his capabilities. He will not mount a direct attack on your strengths. He will look for your vulnerabilities, the places where you do not think defenses are needed.

For example, Satan will not tempt you to hate your family; he will tempt you to absentmindedly let your good deeds consume your time until you are out serving Christ five nights a week. The result for your family will be the same as if you hated them. Mission accomplished.

Defend against Satan's capabilities. As the angel of light, his intentions will appear good. But we must defend against the enemy's capabilities, not his apparent intentions. Protect the jewels Christ entrusted to you.

I SURRENDER

Father, I have been tempted to follow a destructive course. It appeared like a good course, but I didn't weigh all the consequences. I am wrapped up in good intentions. Help me to re-evaluate my priorities. Help me to defend against the schemes of Satan which attack me where I am vulnerable. Never let me think I don't need a strong defense. It is Satan's capabilities against which I must defend, not his apparent good intentions. Amen.

PART EIGHT

Developing My Personal Character

Hot fire makes good steel.

Tommy Boroughs

FORTY-SIX

Suffering: If You Must, Suffer for the Right Reason

It is better, if it is God's will, to suffer for doing good than for doing evil.

1 Peter 3:17

The cold rain drizzled into a mosaic of shallow puddles on the near-empty sidewalk. Menacing cars raced by oblivious to the few pedestrians, each driver absorbed in their own little world. At this early hour, my associate quietly walked beside me down the slumbering street of this strange city while it yawned, and groaned, and stretched to begin another day.

My thoughts tumbled over each other as I pondered what mercy the lender we were walking to meet might show—or not show—me. It had been a foolish decision that I had made, to personally guarantee the loan repayment. Now the major tenant had gone under, and the loan payments could not be met.

Why couldn't I have trusted God more and held firm? Why had I put up additional collateral? The building should have been sufficient to cover the lender's risk. But that was all history now. I had done it on my own. It had been my plan from the very start. I trusted my own ability to make the project work, not God.

Sometimes we suffer at our own hand. Other times we suffer for no apparent reason, and we can't put our finger on why: *Lord, search me again. I can't find anything in me which would cause me to deserve this anguish. What have I done to offend you? How have I failed you? Why do you let me languish in this crucible of bitter gall? Why won't you rescue me from the hands of my adversaries? Please come to me, Lord, please come.*

SHARED SUFFERING

Usually when we suffer, it is for making the wrong choice, but not always. Jesus suffered for doing no wrong. The Lord Jesus never made a wrong choice, yet He was given the vocation of suffering. He did nothing to deserve His destiny.

Because Christ suffered we inherit His kingdom, but to get there we, too, must suffer. We must pass through the gate of sharing in His sufferings. "For it has been granted to you on behalf of Christ not only to believe on him, but also to suffer for him" (Philippians 1:29). Are you surprised to find this passage in the Bible? Does it bother you?

In this age of easy believism, the concept of suffering for Christ seems like a vague abstraction. God assures us we will suffer. "Dear friends, do not be surprised at the painful trial you are suffering, as though something strange were happening to you" (1 Peter 4:12). Persecutions come, illnesses strike, calamities overtake, reverses trample.

In those moments we need a word from the Lord, a touch from the living God. Even when we suffer for doing wrong, we need His touch.

Jesus said, "Do not be afraid of what you are about to suffer" (Revelation 2:10). You will undergo the test, so persevere in doing right, "For it is commendable if a man bears up under the pain of unjust suffering because he is conscious of God" (1 Peter 2:19).

The lender did not show me mercy. I died the agony of a thousand deaths. I suffered for doing wrong. My humiliation before Christ was complete. What devastated me most was not the business loss. What melted my spirit to wax was knowing that I wasn't suffering for the cause of Christ, but for doing wrong. It led to a new level of commitment to obedience. When I suffer again I pray it will be for right, not wrong. If I must suffer, I will at least suffer for the right reason. There is no glory in suffering for doing the wrong thing (see 1 Peter 2:20).

Are you suffering? Is it because you have done right? Or have you fooled yourself and trusted in your own ingenuity? Jesus wants to touch you. He has a word for you. Seek Him, and He will be found. He loves you with an everlasting love. Turn from the way of the world and abandon the plans born of selfish ambition. Do not become weary of suffering because you do good. He will personally care for you in His due time.

I SURRENDER

Lord Jesus, You suffered for doing right. I have suffered because I have done wrong. Revive me to the true gospel. Empower me by the Holy Spirit to abandon my selfish plans. When I suffer again, may it be for the glory of God, for doing good and not wrong. Amen.

FORTY-SEVEN

Character: Circumstance Success Versus Character Success

The Lord was with Joseph and he prospered.

Genesis 39:2

Do you long for the hand of the Lord to prosper you? Does your soul cry out to God for success? Are you baffled by the apparent failure of your circumstances?

The Bible records that God touched many of the heroes of our faith with success—men like Abraham, Jacob, Joseph, David, and Nehemiah. Yet each of these men met with adversities that strained and tested the outer limits of their faith.

Before the Lord prospered Joseph, his brothers severed him from his father and sold him as a slave. After the Lord prospered Joseph in Egypt, he was thrown into prison for a rape that never happened. Just exactly what kind of success is it, then, that Joseph and these other heroes attained? What prosperity does God have in mind?

As a young businessman, God prospered my work far beyond the level I ever desired. Then after fourteen years, He allowed most of it to be taken away. My greatest fear was that no one would like or respect me when my circumstances failed—that no one would love me if I failed. It never happened. Since then, many have told me the way I handled those business problems ministered to others going through similar hard times.

It is not *circumstance* failure which disqualifies you for the friendship, loyalty, and approval of others, but *character* failure. True enough, in the early stages of a circumstance failure, the masses will abandon you, but they were never really with you. But those who love you will stand with you in a surprising, refreshing way.

Later, after you have demonstrated that your character did not fail, people will actually be attracted to you. When your circumstances fail but your character succeeds, you become the model of hope for others. "We know that suffering produces perseverance; perseverance, character; and character, hope. And hope does not disappoint us, because God has poured out his love into our hearts by the Holy Spirit" (Romans 5:3–5).

Why are men and women so devastated when their circumstances fail? Their self-esteem was linked to the success of their circumstances rather than the success of their character. We cannot control our circumstances, but we can control our character. To rely on circumstance success for our self-worth is an open invitation for God to crush that very thing into rubble.

THE FINGERPRINTS OF GOD

When God desires to prosper you, He desires to prosper your character. When God prospers circumstantially, He always does so after character success. When your circumstances succeed and your character fails, God will check. His desire is for our identity to be in Him alone, and not in our circumstances. Any time God observes that your identity is wrapped up in the success of your circumstances, He will humble you.

One day a man shared a pattern of profound spiritual and character growth through which he was going. "Are you going through some hard times?" I asked.

He replied with a surprised look and said, "Why, yes. But what would make you ask that question?"

"Because the period of our greatest character success is often accompanied by the period of our greatest circumstance failure. All the props are knocked away. Christ is the only one left to lean on."

The fingerprints of God are highly visible on the character of a man. When the hands of God knead our spiritual and moral character, He often causes our circumstances to fail. When we depend on our circumstances, the Holy Spirit is grieved. The Holy Spirit is our Guide, our Counselor, our Comforter, our Power. When we abandon Him, He never begs for us to return, rather He changes our circumstances. God is more interested in the success of our character than the success of our circumstances. Does this make sense?

Christ came to prosper you, but in character. He may prosper your circumstances, or He may not. Do not resist Him. "Does not the potter have the right to make out of the same lump of clay some pottery for noble purposes and some for common use?" (Romans 9:21).

Yet regardless of your circumstances, Christ will prosper your character if you will surrender to Him. Joseph led a life as close to a full surrender to God as any human being ever has, and God prospered his character. His circumstances continued to rise and fall, but Joseph found his identity in character success, not circumstance success.

Are you prospering in a material way, or have you been reduced to a pile of rubble? Know that circumstance success is not the goal of a prosperous life. If you succeed in character but fail in circumstances, you succeed overall. If you succeed in circumstances but fail in character, you fail overall. Are you ready to surrender both your character and your circumstances to Christ, who loved you and gave Himself for you?

I Surrender

Dear Father, I confess that I have been measuring my success by my circumstances and not by my character. I have wanted You to prosper my circumstances and bless me in a material way. I now realize Your first priority for my life is character success, not circumstance success. I surrender my circumstances and my character to You right now as an act of faith, trusting You to take my life as a lump of clay and make it what You will. Amen.

FORTY-EIGHT

Tomorrow: The Antidote for Frustration

"Therefore do not worry about tomorrow, for tomorrow will worry about itself."

Matthew 6:34

On peaceful days I feel in absolute accord with the will of Christ. Other times, when a sense of frustration sweeps over me, I am anxious about where Christ is taking my life. The difference always boils down to *trust*, and trust always swirls in the realm of the future.

Are you frustrated about your future? Do you doubt that God's plan is the best plan? I have never doubted that God's plan is the best plan for my life. But I don't always like it. Sometimes a rebellion rises up within me, and I want a break from God's plan—to see things take a different direction.

Do you ever get frustrated because you would like to lead a more important life, a more exciting life, a more rewarding life? These desires are the embers of ambition. God can initiate our ambitions, or we can do it on our own. If you are frustrated, if worry over your plans consumes your thoughts, your ambitions are your own. Yield them to Christ.

Making plans from self-initiated ambition leads to rebellion against the will of God. When once we start a rebellion against the will of God, frustration and worry over tomorrow mark our present. Christ says simply, "Do not worry about tomorrow." It is the antidote for frustration.

FRUSTRATION DEFINED

Frustration for the Christian can be defined as "the extent to which my will does not equal God's will." Whenever we are not *completely* satisfied that the will of God is a sufficient plan for our lives, a sense of panic about the future lunges into our conscious thoughts. "I need a more predictable future, a more concrete plan. I cannot live with this much ambiguity about my life." Christ says, "Do not worry about tomorrow, for tomorrow will worry about itself." By His power He holds all things together, including tomorrow.

Frustration over future plans is a curse. It is a symbol of an unsurrendered life. Jesus promised that the Holy Spirit will teach us all things and remind us of everything Christ told us at the moment of our need. The essence of the Spirit-led life is to take no thought for the morrow. Corrie ten Boom said, "Worry does not empty tomorrow of its sorrow; it empties today of its strength."

Only Christ can resolve the issues of your life. Do you know where the customers are going to come from to meet next month's projections? Do you know how to solve your wife's/husband's restlessness about your marriage? Do you know how to satisfy your craving to lead a meaningful life?

THE ANTIDOTE

Christ is completely trustworthy. Looking back, have you ever been disappointed with the will of God? Although we thought so at the time, we were wrong, for He does not disappoint. He will orchestrate His good, pleasing, and perfect will if we will seek Him as He really is. He says, "Do not worry about tomorrow, for tomorrow will worry about itself. Each day has enough trouble of its own."

The God who is says you will have trouble in this world. "In this world you will have trouble" (John 16:33). The mistaken teaching that once you accept Christ, God will bless you abundantly must be tempered with the reality of the world. "The Scripture declares that the whole world is a prisoner of sin" (Galatians 3:22). The world is the province of the enemy.

Is your life hard right now? Do not be frustrated; God is having His way in your life. Jesus said, "In this world you will have trouble. But take heart! I have overcome the world."

Our hope is not that our plans will work out like we want, but in the tender mercy and grace of Jesus. With Jesus we can face today with His peace. "'I have told you these things, so that in me you may have peace'" (John 16:33). When we stew over our future plans, frustration will sweep over us like a cold, dank fog rolling in from the sea. Dread will replace the innocent trust we were having in Christ. "'Do not worry about tomorrow, for tomorrow will worry about itself.'"

Do you feel like a slave to the future? Does worry over tomorrow consume your thought life? Believe Him when He says tomorrow will worry about itself. Trust Him to take care of you, even if it leads down a hard road. Believe that He has only your best interests in His heart and surrender tomorrow to Him.

He loves you with an everlasting love. Surrender your frustrations and your ambitions to Him. "'Do not worry about tomorrow.'" Live in the present only, and trust tomorrow to the perfection of Christ's promise: "'I have overcome the world'" (John 16:33).

I SURRENDER

Lord Jesus, I have been frustrated about my future, nervous about my life. I confess that I have not trusted tomorrow to You, but I have been seeking to orchestrate my own future. Help me to be content with my life, and to take no thought for the morrow. I will trust You. Amen.

FORTY-NINE

Holiness: Becoming Holy

*Make every effort to live in peace with all men and to
be holy; without holiness no one will see the Lord.*

Hebrews 12:14

Do you ever think, *I have tried to be holy ... but I cannot.
I have given it my best shot, and I simply cannot do it. It is an
impossible task. Others may be able, but I am not. The strain
of trying to be holy is too much; it wears me out.*

A man said recently, "Gosh, I wish I could be like
_____. He seems so committed to the Lord. I find it
impossible to live the Christian life; I'm always messing
up."

The story of the human race is the story of human
weakness and frailty. We strive to be strong, self-suffi-
cient overcomers; we are instead often weak, worn-out,
and weary. We leave a trail of broken relationships and
unkept promises.

Our virtuous motives give way to the fantasies of the
flesh. Our good intentions dissolve in a sea of self-centeredness. Our most noble thoughts occupy the space
immediately adjacent to our most perverted ones. Our
most admirable ambitions suffocate under the avalanche

of the urgent. The juggernaut of the daily press squeezes truth into a once-a-week compartment.

This will never do. We must be holy. The Scriptures state clearly, "without holiness no one will see the Lord." If we cannot be holy, then how will we ever see the Lord? But how can we ever be holy?

WHAT IS HOLINESS?

The holiness we are to exhibit is not our own, but the holiness of Christ in us. We are not holy. We will not become holy humans. Christ in us can manifest His holiness if we will yield our flesh to Him. This is not a human operation, it is spiritual one. Jesus installs His holiness in us by grace. Not a once-for-all-time transaction, this is a daily, moment-by-moment striving to live more by the Spirit and less by the flesh.

Though becoming more holy is God's work in us, it is not a passive enterprise. Our part is active, to strive and strain toward the high calling we have received. God's part is to forgive our failings based on the merit of Christ's atoning death.

His will is that we become holy. "It is God's will that you should be holy" (1 Thessalonians 4:3). This kind of holiness is not the result of our own best effort. Rather, we are to so yield to the Lord Jesus Christ that He can operate as Himself in our lives. His will is that we be holy, but we will be holy only in proportion to how much we yield to the Spirit and not the flesh.

Our problem is that we want to become holy in the same way we want a new car or a raise or a good meal. We want it right now. A friend bought his daughter a new car, but it must sit in the garage until she reaches the legal driving age. Until her sixteenth birthday she only has partial use of the car, when accompanied by an adult. Similarly, holiness is like a gift already purchased for us (by the blood of Christ), but we cannot have full use of it until a certain date in the future (our glorification).

OUR PART

Becoming holy is a process which includes *God's part* and *our part*. On one hand, our part is to stay out of God's part—to yield, to surrender, to stop seeking God on our own terms. But our part also is to obey. It is to enter His rehabilitation program.

When you put yourself under a doctor's care, he cannot help you if you don't follow his instructions. As the patient surrenders his own good ideas and obeys the doctor's instruction, he becomes well. The same is true in sanctification. If you and I want to be made holy, then we must willingly surrender ourselves to His care and we must actively obey His instructions.

We have no more power to make ourselves holy than a dying man can save himself. We are weak and tired, and we cannot offer much help. However, we can submit to His rehabilitation program—sanctification. The key to our part is faith—to seek Him in obedience. "Anyone who comes to him must believe that he exists and that he rewards those who earnestly seek him" (Hebrews 11:6).

If our part is only to have faith, then why do the Scriptures say, "make every effort ... to be holy?" It is because the Scriptures speak of faith actively, not passively. Our effort is the obedience which comes from faith, effort which expresses gratitude for the holiness we freely receive from the merit of Christ.

Satan would have us think our effort makes us holy or, more correctly, that the *failure* of our effort dooms us to be *un*holy. But our sanctification is a process of sin and surrender, over and over again. Holiness is a process of becoming, not a state of being.

GOD'S PART

The forgiveness of Christ makes us holy; He washed away our sin. In reality, God in us—the Holy Spirit—makes us holy. There is no possibility of holiness apart from His grace. He calls us, He justifies us, He sanctifies us (makes us holy), and He will glorify us—all by His grace.

Our part is to surrender in faith; God's part is to implant the sanctifying Holy Spirit in us. "So I say, live by the Spirit, and you will not gratify the desires of the sinful nature" (Galatians 5:16). Because of His everlasting love, we know Him, and He is faithful to mold us into the character of His Son Jesus Christ—to make us holy.

This occurs on an eternal horizon, not a temporal one. So as you and I take a few temporal steps and fall, like a toddler learning to walk, our loving Father exhorts us to make the effort to get up and try again—by yielding to the process of His sanctification. When we leave the world that is passing away and enter the kingdom of heaven, we will take full possession of our holiness.

I SURRENDER

Father, I long deeply to be different, to be holy as Christ is holy. I confess I have focused on my own effort and not the enabling of Your Holy Spirit. I surrender myself completely to Your will, "that I should be holy." Now have Your own way with me as I wobble along for these next few steps. Your love compels me to try again. Amen.

FIFTY

Equipping: The Lag from Calling to Sending

*Then after three years, I went up to Jerusalem to get
acquainted with Peter and stayed with him fifteen days.*

Galatians 1:18

Do you sense that God has called you to something, but
you don't know what? There is always a lag between the
calling and the sending of a saint. What is the thing from
the old you that still persists, even though you now have
Christ? That is what God must work on (to add or subtract) before He sends you. First, He calls. Then, He
equips. Then, He sends.

It is hard to be called by God and to live in our society
at the same time. In America, when the action impulse
comes, action follows immediately. No patience required—
technology and culture let us proceed immediately. Not so
with God. Immediately when He calls us, He postpones
our sending. There is other work to be done first.

THE CALLING, EQUIPPING, AND SENDING OF PAUL

The Apostle Paul experienced the most dramatic conversion in all of history. On the road to Damascus, a light

suddenly flashed, and he fell to the ground. Jesus said to him, "'Saul, Saul, why do you persecute me?'" (Acts 9:4). For three days Paul stumbled around blind and did not eat or drink. Then God sent Ananias to Paul to deliver this calling: "'This man is my chosen instrument to carry my name before the Gentiles and their kings and before the people of Israel'" (Acts 9:15).

Immediately upon hearing it, Paul began to preach that Jesus is the Son of God. The people were astonished, and he grew more and more powerful in his calling. Then an odd thing happened. After only a few days, Paul fled to Arabia where he remained in obscurity for three years. Here was a famous man, the persecutor of the Christians, known throughout the region, feared by every Christian. His conversion would be big news. His calling to take the gospel to the Gentiles would be very big news indeed. But he was not ready for his calling.

God caused a lag between the calling and the sending of Paul. God took Paul to the desert for three years because there was something that God still needed to work into—or out of—Paul. Only God knew what it was for Paul. What is it for you? Or do you know yet? It is not all that important that you even know what God is doing in you. Knowing that He is the one doing it should suffice.

To know that God causes the lag between our calling and our sending is satisfying. He always equips us for the calling before the sending. He will never give us a task for which we are not sufficiently equipped. We can, of course, go before we are actually sent. This is the work of the flesh, and it always results in a delay.

We need the lag between our calling and our sending for God to do His repair work on us. He wants to send only properly prepared people. We must allow enough time to do it right the first time.

A CHANGE OF CALLING

When a new calling comes, the sense of purpose we had from our previous calling withers away. Instead of feeling a surge of power and confidence about the future, the future becomes an unfocused blur. The natural reaction is to make a plan of our own, to set some new goals. The spiritual reaction is to thank God for the blur. It is a time for God to work that thing in or out of your life. It is a time of tearing down old thinking and building up new thinking. It is a time to abandon the inevitable presuppositions and self-deceit that build up over time. It is a time for self-examination. It is a time to be re-equipped.

The lag between the calling and the sending should be a sweet time, a special time. It is a time for reflection, for rededication, for renewal. Don't be rushed into the sending. God will reveal that day with an unmistakable signal. No doubt will remain that it is the sending time. "Then after three years, I went up to Jerusalem to get acquainted with Peter" (Galatians 1:18).

Are you called but not sent? Know that God causes the lag between the calling and the sending of a saint. He equips and prunes during the lag. These can be the most precious moments of personal relationship with Christ—if you don't keep insisting that it's time to be sent. Relax. Be patient. Wait upon Him. Wait for His unmistakable signal, but you don't need to worry that you will miss it. You will not. God will not let you.

I SURRENDER

Dear God, I confess that I have been frustrated with my life. I have been called but not sent, and I have resisted, even resented, the lack of direction in my life. Help me to relax and enjoy the lag. And show me the thing(s) to add and subtract. Amen.

FIFTY-ONE

Isolation: Stuck on a Blank Page

My soul thirsts for God, for the living God. When can I go and meet with God?

Psalm 42:2

It was a frigid morning. My breath fogged the inside window of the cab as I peered out at the tall buildings soaring above the crowded, bustling streets of New York City. I hadn't slept very well. The reflection of my face in the window stared back, and I thought how fatigued I must look.

In less than ten minutes, I would walk into a meeting upon which my entire financial fate hinged. Months and months of negotiations had boiled down to two or three remaining issues. Those settled, we had a deal. Left unsettled, disaster and certain ruin held the mortgage on my future. And it looked pretty unsettled at the moment. *Why me?* I wondered.

For months-on-end my life had become a robotic exercise of getting up, ritualistically going through the motions of the day, and then collapsing in mental and emotional exhaustion. I was stuck on a blank page between the chapters of my life.

When is the last time you were stuck on a blank page? Why does God so often leave us there. We shrivel up, feeling isolated from Him, not sensing His presence, immobilized by our circumstances. Where is He when we need Him?

God is always there when we need Him. The problem, of course, is that we are not always there when we need Him. When we are deep in the middle of a pot-boiling chapter of our life, we are too busy for Him.

Be sure of this: Whenever a chapter of your life drives you to distraction from your personal relationship with Christ, a blank page is just ahead. He stops us cold. He abruptly places an obstacle in our path. He throws our private life into disarray.

God makes us thirst for Him. He will send you to the thirsty desert of a blank page. His highest desire is that we would long for a personal relationship with Him, as a perishing prospector pines for a drink of water. "As the deer pants for streams of water, so my soul pants for you, O God" (Psalm 42:1).

He will never let you go, even if it means you stay stuck on the blank page. Picture a rebellious child trying to run away from home. The father restrains, disciplines, chastens, and restricts. What father would give up on his son? Nor will God give up on you. Love, not hatred, leads to the blank page.

When it seems as though He has forgotten you, that you will be stuck forever on that page, in the end you look for Him. You ask, "When can I go and meet with God?" That is the purpose of the blank page.

Have you been so busy with your life that He has brought you to a screeching halt? Have His waves and breakers swept over you? Is the pressure building? The unsurrendered life is the precursor of a blank page.

Thirst for God and you will be filled. When your problems exceed your ingenuity, God is reestablishing the personal relationship. He knows a blank page will bring you back to surrender. "The righteous cry out and the Lord hears them; he delivers them from all their troubles. The Lord is close to the brokenhearted and saves those who are crushed in spirit. A righteous man may have many troubles, but the Lord delivers him from them all" (Psalm 37:17–19).

As I walked into the ornate board room, eyes darted knowingly among the assembled parties. After a while, it became apparent they thought their best interests would be served by making the deal work. So it worked. I was grateful.

On the cab ride back to the airport, I noticed the sun shined brightly through the clear, bracing air of a crisp winter afternoon. I hadn't noticed earlier. I even heard some birds chirping as we crossed Park Avenue. I did not feel thirsty anymore. "God, how I love having a *personal* relationship with you."

I SURRENDER

Dear God, I am embroiled in this chapter of my life. I confess it has become a real pot-boiler. Things are coming apart. I have not been thinking much about my personal relationship with You. I have been rebellious, and You have put me on a blank page. Let my soul thirst for You, the living God. I surrender these next weeks and months (or however long it takes) to reestablish our personal relationship. Amen.

FIFTY-TWO

Sorrow: The Food and Drink of Job

*"The Lord gave and the Lord has taken away; may the
name of the Lord be praised."*

Job 1:21

Sooner or later we all identify with Job. Few of us will
ever suffer the depths which swallowed up his life. The
torment which consumed him, and more specifically his
response, involuntarily draws us toward him. What is it
about Job with which we so identify?

God exalted Job's character to Satan. Satan then
accused, "Does Job fear God for nothing?" For Job was
the greatest man among his people. So God permitted
Job's testing and, in the process, he lost all of his wealth,
his business, his family, and finally his health.

What is it about this tragic story that captivates our
interest? It is Job's response—his undaunted response.
Deep in every human breast we long to have the courage
and character of Job. He is the quintessential Christian.
He lived a blameless and upright life, fearing God and
shunning evil. He was a godly person and Job did not

buckle when the juggernaut of life crushed him beneath its wheels.

The question which taxes our limits is, "Why?" Why did God allow Satan to consume the life of a "blameless and upright" man? The story of Job doesn't give up that answer, and that is not the story's point. This story is not rendered to help us understand how God works, but how man responds. It is not a story about the *cause* of sorrow, but our *response* to sorrow. This story is about submitting to the sovereign will of God.

FAITH AND COURAGE

Job is God's gift to us to buttress our faith and courage. He transfuses hope into our bloodstream. Job becomes our food and drink. We eat him up, and slowly our own strength begins to return. He models the perfect response to the tragedies and heartaches which, sooner or later, befall us all. He is not perfect in the sense that he is without error, but perfect in that his faith in the Almighty never wavered. He is the paragon of faith. If anything, Job's faith burgeoned. "Naked I came from my mother's womb, and naked I will depart. The Lord gave and the Lord has taken away; may the name of the Lord be praised." (Job 1:21).

To see one man defeat Satan proves that he can be defeated. If you cling to the integrity of God—His promised mercy and grace, then you can face a Job-like trial. You can taste the same pain and not be consumed. You can defeat the defeatable foe. Say to your calamities, "The Lord gave and the Lord has taken away; may the name of the Lord be praised." Do not accuse God so that you, like Job, will also remain blameless. "In all this, Job did not sin by charging God with wrongdoing" (Job 1:22).

HOPE

Job is God's gift to stir the embers of hope in our hearts when waves of despair douse the flames of our enthusiasm. His courage *en*courages us—it inspires us to have courage.

Job was like us. He could not hold his tongue during the anguish of his testing. He spewed forth his own understanding of the nature of things, and in this he sinned. God reprimanded him, Job repented, and God accepted him. God loves contrite people.

"The Lord blessed the latter part of Job's life more than the first" (Job 42:12). God made "him prosperous again and gave him twice as much as he had before" (Job 42:10). This is a glorious outcome, but it is not our hope. This is what God did for Job; He may or may not do it for you.

Our hope is not to gain prosperity, but to gain Christ. Job doesn't model enduring pain for an expected outcome, but to show us how to respond to tragedy. In due time God restores, but sovereignly. Surrender your expectations to God, and wait patiently for Him to restore you. Our hope is Christ.

Our faith and courage will sustain us. Even on the days when we are so bone-tired weary, so completely and totally fatigued that we don't know how we can go on, the thought of Job can be our food and drink. His paragon will help sustain our maltreated minds, our broken bodies, and our sorrowful souls.

Do not rage at God over the injustice which besets you, even if it consumes your wealth, your career, your family, your health. God always works these things together for good when you, like Job, are called according to His purpose. Every good thing you have—or had—comes from the hand of God. So if you are separated from good things, fall to the ground in worship. Join with Job and say, "The Lord gave and the Lord has taken away; may the name of the Lord be praised."

I SURRENDER

Dear God, I am weary. Circumstances have doused the flickering flame of hope I held for my future. The waves of what You have caused or allowed have swept over me. I confess I have accused You of wrongdoing. Forgive me. I confess that I have thought more about why You would let this happen to me than about how to properly respond. Forgive me. My tortured soul feels the anguish of a life that isn't turning out like I planned. But I know that You give and You take away. Therefore I say, blessed is the name of the Lord. Amen.

FIFTY-THREE

Trust: Trust God with All Your Heart

Trust in the Lord with all your heart and lean not on your own understanding.

Proverbs 3:5

A sales executive I know constantly sulks, whimpers, and whines over his mediocre sales performance. He presumes those who earn a better living than he does must engage in some sort of spurious practices. He masks his disappointment with that common refrain, "I'm just trusting in the Lord."

This man constantly rehearses the faults of more successful people in his field to make himself feel better. He has not opened a trade magazine or attended a seminar in years; he isn't motivated to gain a first-rate understanding of his product and develop new applications for his customers. He, like many people only "trust the Lord" to cover up for mediocrity.

If any one point of the Bible repeats itself more than the rest, it must be this idea of trusting God. "Trust ... and lean not on your own understanding." Does this mean we fly blind? Of course not.

Implicit in not leaning on your understanding is that you have taken the time to build an understanding upon which you do not rely. God doesn't want bumbling businessmen or ho-hum housewives who don't develop the most excellent understanding of their field possible.

God says to trust Him. He also says don't lean, or depend, on your own understanding. To not lean on it, you must have one. The idea of blind trust miscues what God is saying. He wants us to build the finest understanding of whatever field we pursue, whether science, business, theology, the arts, music, medicine or anything else.

And don't think home-making isn't major league to God:

> The most creative job in the world involves fashion, decorating, recreation, education, transportation, psychology, romance, cuisine, literature, art, economics, government, pediatrics, geriatrics, entertainment, maintenance, purchasing, law, religion, energy, and management. Anyone who can handle all those has to be somebody special. She is. She's a homemaker. (Richard Kerr)

Be excellent, the very best you can be. God loves experts. They bring Him honor.

THE RISK

The risk is to understand so well that we stop trusting. It is a delicate balance. Learn everything you can, but always trust the Lord for direction. Trust Him with one hundred percent of your heart, soul, mind, and strength.

Once we use every reasonable effort to understand our situation and give our personal best, then we fret not one iota over the outcome, but "trust in the Lord." By looking to God as the source of our supply and not to men, we fulfill the challenge: "In all your ways acknowledge him, and he will make your paths straight" (Proverbs 3:6).

I Surrender

My Father, I confess I have used the principle of trusting in You to condone the mediocre effort I have been putting forth. I ask You to give me the strength and courage to develop the best possible understanding of every task and responsibility for which I am entrusted. Help me become excellent. Even though I may achieve a superior understanding, I will always surrender the outcome to my trust in the Lord. Amen.

FIFTY-FOUR

Surrender: The Prayer of Agur

"Two things I ask of you, O Lord; do not refuse me before I die."

Proverbs 30:7

The first several dozen times I read the prayer of Agur I thought it was good for Agur but anathema for me. I could never pray it.

What is the prayer of Agur? "Two things I ask of you, O Lord; do not refuse me before I die: Keep falsehood and lies far from me" (Proverbs 30:7–8). So far so good. This first request is no more than a prayer for integrity. What Christian doesn't want to have integrity? No matter how steeped in sin a Christian becomes, he always wants to flee from immorality when he comes to his senses.

The second part of Agur's prayer strikes a different cord: "Give me neither poverty nor riches, but give me only my daily bread" (Proverbs 30:8).

Lord, I have built my whole life around integrity. But my goal has always been to become financially independent. I cannot pray this prayer. It may be good for Agur, but it's certainly not for me.

The barely audible voice of memory whispers, "Give us today our daily bread" (Matthew 6:11).

I don't like that prayer either, Lord.

Two Great Tests

Integrity and Money are two great tests. The test of integrity appeals to our logic, it enhances our reputation among people. When we are moral our esteem rises. Perhaps that is why Agur did not sense the need to amplify his prayer for integrity. The test of money goes against our logic. To pray against riches is to pray against everything we have been working toward.

Maybe that is why Agur sensed the need to amplify his prayer that God would give him "neither poverty nor riches. He explained, " Otherwise, I may have too much and disown you and say, 'Who is the Lord?' Or I may become poor and steal, and so dishonor the name of my God" (Proverbs 30:9).

Have you ever had "too much"? The test of prosperity is greater than the test of poverty, though they are both telling tests.

You and I have a curse. The curse is that we believe we can handle riches where weaker men cannot. We think we can handle more money and not forget God. The plain truth is that we already have too much. If we are completely honest, we must admit that the riches we already have, however little they may be, cause us to drift away from the things of God. The possessions we already have consume us. The time it takes to manage what we already have makes us act as if we don't know the Lord, even if we never consciously say, "Who is the Lord?"

Money competes with God, while integrity complements God. Money is the greater test, for it is the dominant value of a world that is passing away. Honoring Christ is the dominant value of the world that is coming, and the prayer of Agur seeks to honor Christ.

I have learned to prayed the prayer of Agur (and mean it). Like most of us, I have had "too much." It took several years to surrender to the point I could pray for neither poverty nor riches. Where are you on your pilgrimage? Are you secure enough with Christ to pray the prayer of Agur?

I SURRENDER

"Two things I ask of you, O Lord; do not refuse me before I die: Keep falsehood and lies far from me; give me neither poverty nor riches, but give me only my daily bread. Otherwise, I may have too much and disown You and say, 'Who is the Lord?' Or I may become poor and steal, and so dishonor the name of my God." Amen.

FIFTY-FIVE

Human Nature:
The Weaknesses We
Detest in Others

So I find this law at work: When I want to do good,
evil is right there with me.

Romans 7:21

We all piled into our boat for a Fourth of July family outing. As we navigated through a narrow, tropical canal, another boat—a bigger boat—approached from the other direction. Isn't it interesting that no matter how big your boat, there is always someone with a bigger one?

I watched the captain of this seaworthy ship standing proudly erect in the center of his bow, hands clasped behind his back. His family scurried around to make sure our boats passed safely in the canal. But the icy captain stood sternly at the bow—cool, calm, and collected.

As our boats closed on each other I was sure I detected the trace of a snobbish sneer on his face. *Yes, there it is again! He is glaring smugly down on us because he has a bigger boat. What haughtiness, sheer arrogance,* I thought to myself, *I could care less.*

The sin of pride is a sin of comparison, comparing our strength to another's weakness. For most of us, our greatest strengths are usually also our greatest weaknesses.

I stewed over this boater's self-importance. Sure, I could have owned a bigger boat, but my restrained lifestyle was a strength of mine. Then it hit me hard. It was not his pride that was at issue with Christ; it was mine. I was the proud fool.

The first choice of my human nature was to charge him with pride, of comparing his strength (his big boat) to my weakness (my little boat). But it was me that was guilty of pride, of comparing my strength (my restrained lifestyle) with his weakness (his consumptive lifestyle).

AN AXIOM TO LIVE BY

Any time our ire rises at the sin of someone else, a sin is revealed in us, often the same sin. We detest in others the weaknesses and sins we have not yet sorted out in ourselves.

The nature of our human nature is to remember the positive things about ourselves, and note all the negative things about the other person. We remember our strengths, and note their weaknesses—not always, but often.

When we assume ourselves to be a good person at the level of our basic human nature, we set ourselves up for a fall. "There is no one righteous, not even one" (Romans 3:10). Each of us is capable of committing any particular sin at any particular time.

The best defense we have is to acknowledge our basic human nature—not good but sinful—and leave a sentinel posted at the gate to our mind. "Take captive every thought to make it obedient to Christ" (2 Corinthians 10:5). Then we will not be caught unaware by the soft sell of sin's seductions at the level of our basic human nature.

Man is capable of doing great good, but always by the grace of God, and always with the capacity to do evil right there with him.

Will we ever attain a complete victory over the nature of our human nature? Will we ever be free from the shackles of our own inclination to sin? The answer is no, not in this life. We must live with this ambiguity: "When I want do good, evil is right there with me" (Romans 7:21).

I SURRENDER

Dear God, now that I belong to You, let me live my life by the Spirit. Help me to become unconvinced of my own goodness at the level of my basic human nature. I see how the sins I hate in others are often my own. I surrender my sinful nature to You. Help me to overcome the ambiguity within me. Amen.

FIFTY-SIX

Pressure: The Purpose of Pressure

We were under great pressure, far beyond our ability to endure, so that we despaired even of life.

2 Corinthians 1:8

Everyone is busy. Some people just don't talk about it as much as others. It is true that some people are busier than others but, still, everyone these days has a lot to do. Busyness puts us all under a load of pressure.

When the pressure on you mounts, how do you decide which way to go, which priorities you will pursue? How do you choose when there is job pressure, financial pressure, family pressure, pressure to do church and ministry work, and pressure to take some time off? How about pressure to compromise, to get angry, to lead a secret thought life? Or the pressure that takes you away from walking closely with God?

The Apostle Paul burned up as much energy as anyone—he was a busy man. At one point he vulnerably wrote to Corinth that he felt so much pressure that "we despaired even of life." What solace to know that even imperturbable Paul experienced this common human emotion.

What is the purpose of pressure? Why do we feel the great pressures, even to the point of despair? Paul explains the purpose of our pressure by explaining the purpose of his own: "But this happened that we might not rely on ourselves but on God" (2 Corinthians 1:9).

The purpose of pressure is to keep us constantly dependent upon the Lord Jesus. The Lord Jesus is our rescue, our guide, our Master. To rely on Him is to please the Father. When we rely upon ourselves, He cannot deliver us. When we yield to Him, He can deliver us. "He has delivered us . . . , and he *will* deliver us" (2 Corinthians 1:10, emphasis added).

Our experience of delivery is the empirical evidence that His Word is true. Has He delivered you once? It is our assurance that He will deliver us again.

I SURRENDER

Lord Jesus, I am busy. The burden of my pressure weighs down on me like a heavy load. Use this to redirect my dependency to You. Slow me down, Lord. I do not want to rely on myself but on the power of God. Deliver me again, I pray. I will rely upon You. Amen.

FIFTY-SEVEN

Service: The Reward for Serving Others

Serve wholeheartedly, as if you were serving the Lord, not men, because you know that the Lord will reward everyone for whatever good he does.

Ephesians 6:7–8

I met Bill quite by chance, or at least I thought so at the time. I could tell he was living in a hard place; it was in his eyes. So conspicuous was the agony that when I would shut my own eyes, I would see his. I could barely concentrate on anything else for several days. One morning we had a cup of coffee together, and God used the time to minister to us both.

His wife had divorced him, he had lost his job, he couldn't find meaningful work, his self-image was shot, he was depressed, and his Christian friends had dropped him.

He deeply appreciated the time I spent with him, then and over the next several months. All those months I could tell he was watching me closely, to see how I lived, to find out who I really was, to see if I was for real. In short, he wanted to see if I was as good as my first impression.

I am not. I am weak. If someone observes for too long, my "other" foot will protrude. I cannot bear such close scrutiny. I will disappoint everyone in my life—usually sooner than later. It is the same with you, and with Bill, and with all of us.

Before too long I let Bill down. I didn't last as the warm, interested friend. What Bill couldn't see, of course, was that I had problems of my own, priorities left unattended in my own life, human frailties and weaknesses of my own.

TWO PROBLEMS, SAME SOLUTION

Two great problems in serving others are both problems of the human nature, of focusing on our relationships with people instead of our relationship with Christ. The first problem is that people will expect too much of you; and the second, you will expect too much of them. Both of these problems are problems of unrealistic expectations. Expectations must be focused on Christ, not each other. He is the only One who will consistently not let us down.

The milk of human sympathy will undernourish your soul. No amount of human gratitude will properly compensate your effort to improve the human condition. When we focus on serving the person, we are inevitably disappointed. And what's more, we will disappoint them. Serving people for the sake of their gratitude is a guaranteed formula for disappointment. Just when you begin to feel good about your labors, someone lets you down. Or, more likely, someone will expect too much from you and accuse you of letting them down. Either way, your destiny is to be terribly discouraged.

Why do Christians shrink from serving others with zeal? Every time the Christian gives of himself in service and the recipient still isn't satisfied, his spirit withers a bit more. We wonder, "Why bother?" The ingratitude is harsh. The issue is to clarify *why* we serve, not whimper over ingratitude from *whom* we serve. Our motive must be to please God, not men.

The key is the personal relationship with Christ. The focus must not be on serving others or on being served. The focus must be on Jesus, on becoming so absorbed in the relationship with Him that every other thing is a response to our relationship. We don't serve men; we serve God. Have no expectations of men. Focus on the personal relationship with Him, and there will be an overflow available for others.

THE REWARD

Look to Christ alone for gratitude. If you serve Christ, then you will remember to look to Him for your approval, not to the milk of human sympathy. He will reward you for serving others; in fact, He is the reward.

When someone feels you let them down, you can surrender that relationship to Christ. You are serving Him only; He will give you the strength to serve that same person more. You may want to flee from the ingratitude—the insatiable demands of other people—but Christ will empower you to be a servant if you take on His attitude. It can only come by devotion to the personal relationship.

The personal relationship with Christ is the oasis in the desert of human relations. When people begin to wear you down, let it remind you that you are not in the overflow. It is time to drink of Christ.

Are you beat down because your service has not been appreciated? Have you been looking for the milk of human sympathy? Go to Him and be filled to overflow. Then you can serve with gratitude. Your expectations will be supernatural, not natural.

I SURRENDER

Father, I have been discouraged by people. They have demanded much and given little in return. I confess I have done my good deeds for them instead of You. I have also let people down. Help me to heal the wounds which come from the unrealistic expectations others have of me. Remove the alternating guilt and anger I feel toward those who demand much but give little. Help me to do my service for Your approval only. Amen.

Discussion Leader's Guide

Use a devotional book for a men's small group? Definitely! A devotional book is great for a new small group, especially for men who may be new to the whole "small group experience." This book will make it easy to lead a group as well. Any man interested in starting a group to discuss *Devotions for the Man in the Mirror* can successfully lead a lively discussion by following these guidelines:

1. Decide how many weeks your group will meet and pick the chapters to read and discuss each week. Groups may be existing Bible studies, fellowship groups, prayer groups, or Sunday school classes (women can be included). Or, you may want to start a new group. Don't try and make guys commit to meeting fifty-seven times. That may be overwhelming. Just agree to meet for anywhere from six to twelve weeks. Then each guy can decide at that time whether he wants to continue.

2. How to Start a New Group: Photostat the Table of Contents and give a copy to the men you want to meet with. Ask them if they would like to be in a discussion group that would read the book and discuss how the issues raised affect their lives. This can be a group from work, church, your neighborhood, or a combination. The optimum-sized group would be eight to twelve men (assuming some men will have to miss a week occasionally).

3. First Week: Distribute a copy of the book to each member together with a typed schedule. Assign the

first chapter as next week's reading assignment and ask them to be prepared to share a thought or two about what they read. Then go around the room and ask each man to share with the group where he is on his spiritual pilgrimage. This is a great icebreaker, and the men will be encouraged, and will enjoy learning about where other men are on their pilgrimage. Be sure to point out that there are no wrong answers to this question. Some may just be starting on their pilgrimage, others may be well down the road. Close with a prayer. Always adjourn exactly when you said you would.

4. Typical Week: Begin with an icebreaker question. As an alternative, you may ask a different man each week to give a maximum five-minute personal testimony of how he became a Christian. During a one-hour meeting a good schedule to follow would be:

- Icebreaker question—5 minutes
- Discussion of chapter—45 minutes
- Group prayer—10 minutes

5. Alternative Typical Week: Prepare a twenty-minute lecture based on the chapter. After your presentation, spend thirty minutes discussing the questions and ten minutes in prayer. Use your creativity to think of other ways to help men deal with the man in the mirror. Or, ask each man to take a week to present the chapter and come up with two or three discussion questions of his own for the group.

6. Have coffee and soft drinks available. If you meet over lunch or breakfast, allow an extra fifteen minutes for eating, if possible.

7. Leading a Discussion: The key to a successful discussion group will be your ability to ensure that each member gets "air time." Your role is to encourage each man to render his thoughts and ideas on the subject of the day. If off-the-subject questions are asked, simply suggest that you discuss that at a separate time. If someone rambles too much, privately ask them to help you draw out the more shy members of the group.

8. You don't have to be an experienced Bible teacher to lead a discussion using *Devotions for the Man in the Mirror*. If someone asks you a question beyond your scope, simply say so and move on.

9. Be creative; there is no single "right" way to have a men's discussion group.

The pleasure and added understanding you will experience from a group discussion will prove to be well worth the effort on your part.

About the Author

Since the late 1980s, Patrick Morley has been one of America's most respected authorities on the unique challenges and opportunities that men face. After spending the first part of his career in the highly competitive world of commercial real estate, Patrick has been used throughout the world to help men think more deeply about their lives.

In 1973 Patrick founded Morley Properties, which for several years was hailed as one of Florida's one hundred largest privately held companies. During this time he was the president or managing partner of fifty-nine companies and partnerships. In 1989 he wrote *The Man in the Mirror*, a landmark book that poured from his own search for meaning, purpose, and a deeper relationship with God. This bestselling book captured the imaginations of hundreds of thousands of men worldwide. As a result, in 1991 Patrick Morley sold his business and founded Man in the Mirror, a ministry to men. Through his speaking and writing, he has become a tireless advocate for men, encouraging and inspiring them to change their lives in Christ. He has authored eleven books, most recently, *The Young Man in the Mirror* and *The Dad in the Mirror*, coauthored with David Delk.

"Our ministry exists," says Patrick Morley, "in answer to the prayers of all those wives, mothers, and grandmothers who have for decades been praying for the men in their lives."

Man in the Mirror's faculty members conduct church sponsored men's events nationwide. Patrick's dream is to network with other ministries and churches of all denominations to reach every man in America with a credible offer of salvation and the resources to grow in Christ. To that end, he chairs the Steering Committee for the National Coalition of Men's Ministries.

Patrick Morley graduated with honors from the University of Central Florida, earned a master's degree from Reformed Theological Seminary, and has completed studies at Oxford and the Harvard Business School.

Every Friday morning, Patrick teaches a Bible study to 150 businessmen in Orlando, Florida, where he lives with his wife, Patsy. Their two married children live in Missouri and in Alabama.

Want to read more by
Patrick Morley?

A Patrick Morley Reading Guide for Men

Want to Reinvent
Yourself?

Want a Success That
Really Matters?

Personal
Reflections

For Men in
Transition

*Man in the
Mirror* Workbook

Practical
Direction

A Compelling
Evangelism Tool

We want to hear from you. Please send your
comments about this book to us in care of
zreview@zondervan.com. Thank you.

GRAND RAPIDS, MICHIGAN 49530 USA

WWW.ZONDERVAN.COM

Through the generosity of our publisher Zondervan, our donors, and strategic partners, Man in the Mirror is able to make this book available to you.